M000317973

A COMPILATION OF WOMEN NONPROFIT EXECUTIVES

THE
NONPROFIT
LEGACY

TAJALA BATTLE-LOCKHART

AWARD-WINNING NONPROFIT EXECUTIVES

A COMPILATION OF EXPERTS

THE NONPROFIT
LEGACY

Printed in the United States of America
Copyright @ 2020 Tajala Battle-Lockhart

ISBN: 978-1-7357089-4-2

Library of Congress Cataloging-in-Publication Data

The copyright laws of the United States of America protect this book.
No part of this publication may be reproduced or stored electronically or
otherwise transmitted in any form or by any means (electronic, photocopy,
recording) without written permission of the author or for commercial gain or
profit.

Scripture quotations: Taken from the Holy Bible: New Living Translation
(NLT). Wheaton, Ill: Tyndale House Publishers, 2004 and The King
James Version. Dallas, Brown Books Publishing, 2004.

Professional Editing: SynergyEd Consulting/ synergyedconsulting.com

Graphics & Book Layout: Greenlight Creations Graphics Designs

Cover Design: Greenlight Creations - glightcreations.com/
glightcreations@gmail.com

Publishing & Marketing: SHERO Publishing.com

shero
publishing

getpublished@sheropublishing.com

SHEROPUBLISHING.COM

TABLE OF CONTENTS

AUTHOR CHAPTERS

Dedication

This book is dedicated to those community warriors who want to serve and develop successful nonprofits. It will serve as a blueprint for future leaders and village workers who want honest feedback, are committed to do the hard work that's required, and want tools that will support and guide them in the right direction to build sustainable nonprofits. The book is not a guarantee of success; leaders must be willing to do the hard work, the necessary research, and invest in the organizations. The book is a tangible support tool that provides interested individuals access to the nonprofit leaders in this compilation who will help them get through this journey. In addition, it serves as a reminder that when you collaborate with others, you can definitely make a greater impact in your community and the world.

Dedication to Co-Authors:

To all the amazing co-authors that said "yes" to this project, I have thanked you throughout this entire journey. I am so honored that you chose to be a part of this project with me. I am grateful that God blessed me with each and every one of you. I am so blessed to connect and collaborate with you all. Thank you for sharing your heart, tears, and stories along the way.

Thanks to the phenomenal SHERO Publishing team; especially our amazing Coaches Kimberly Perry Sanderlin, Camilla Moore and founder, Erica Perry Green. You ladies made this book compilation such an amazing experience.

In Tribute To

In Honor of:

I am dedicating this book to the woman who inspired my nonprofit: my beautiful mother. She was a single mom that worked so hard to give me that best that she had to offer. She had a big heart; however, she was definitely a rose that wore her thorns to protect those around her. However, she never focused on protecting herself, so I decided to take on the role of her protector. She was my everything: my mom, my friend and everything that I have done in my life is to make her proud. Mommy this is for you! This is my first book and I am pouring into others just as you, my grandmother (Ma Dear) did, and as you taught me to do! I love you to life and I hope you're pleased with all that I have accomplished since you've been gone. My Forever Rose!!

Acknowledgments

I would like to acknowledge my husband, Derrick Lockhart, for understanding and supporting my passion for serving my community in so many different ways. You get frustrated sometimes due to the time, money, and the commitment it takes; however, you have never tried to discourage me to stop because you have seen the impact that it makes on the people that I serve.

To my sweet daughter, Chelsey Lockhart, thank you for sharing your mom with other young women. Most children don't understand, but you show me that you understand why mommy does this work. As a result, I see you doing the same thing too for others. This is all for you. I am preparing a safe place for you, so you can have a community of sisterhood: family to comfort you in your time of need. This is my legacy that I want to leave behind for you. I want you to see that I want nothing but protection, safety, warmth, and love surrounding you; whether I am near or far. My sweet Chelsey, thank you so much, my love. You mean the world to me and this is all for you.

To my Aunt Carolyn Williams and Aunt Ann Smith, you ladies are my forever Angels. You were there in my greatest time of need and you gave it your all. I want to take this time to share with you that without your strength, support, and courage, I would not have been able to accomplish all that I have to date. Thank you for caring for my mom until her last day. I am and will forever be grateful for each of you because you could have easily ignored her needs and focused on your own. That's never been your spirit and I thank you for providing her the gift of true sisterhood.

To Mrs. Billie Harley and Mrs. Mary Mangino, you ladies are my Angels and I am forever grateful to you. You ladies are our silent cheerleaders. We love you ladies so much for all you do for PYW.

To all the parents and young women that continue to trust PYW with your growth and safety, we continue to be committed to you. We are forever grateful to you for your trust and support.

To every volunteer and guest speaker, we truly appreciate and value the time and commitment you gave or will give to PYW. To every donor that has financially poured into PYW without you, there would be no PYW. Thank you for investing in our mission to support the building of young women in our community.

To Andrea Pope-Matheson, my sister/friend without you, PYW would not have been able to continue on. It started with your- "Yes" when others walked away. Your dedication made it possible for PYW to be here today. Thank you for believing in my vision and mission and being willing to take on such a great commitment to build young women in our community. Our moms would be so proud to stand with us if they were here. Let's see what the future holds!

To the most amazing man who was willing to fulfill my dream of having a father, Mr. Eirthly Govan; know that I am grateful. Your gift of love and being a grandfather to Chelsey is priceless. You were God's greatest gift to me! I love you to life!

Foreword Contributor
Tanya Barnett:

Tanya is a 100% permanent and total disabled veteran, women veterans advocate, LGBTQIA+ ally, and an adjunct professor. Tanya has advocated on the behalf of women veterans to the United States Congress as well as to audiences around the United States.

Tanya served in the Air Force at Lackland Air Force Base in Wilford Hall Medical Center from 1993-1997, where she was an Obstetrical Intensive Care Unit and Labor & Delivery Technician, She also worked in the operating room, surgical clinic, and the emergency room.

While working with the sickest pregnant women in the military, Tanya realized early on that she had a calling to assist women in need. After witnessing several patients die during childbirth, she implemented a program that trained other Obstetrical Intensive Care Unit and Labor & Delivery technicians to honor their deceased patients and their families. In 1994, she was the only Airman in her division to receive a 59th Medical Wing commander coin and several citations for her innovative program.

Tanya is a 2018 *N.A.A.C.P. Hall of Famer* and the 2016 *Charles County Citizen of the Year* for the work of Forever Free Books, the nonprofit she and her husband founded in 2014. They deliver free books and conduct storytime to low-income children in their communities. To reduce the literacy gap between wealthy children and low-income children, they intentionally bring African American men into underserved communities to expose them to college-educated men who read to them. Sadly, they dissolved their nonprofit in 2020 due to Tanya experiencing a stroke. Because of this, she is dedicated to ensuring there will be public policies in place that support women and their families so that she can reduce the number of women who experience strokes and other health issues related to stress.

Tanya is also the award-winning, self-published author of *Being a Wife Just Got Real, Things I Wish I Knew Before I Said, "I Do", You Need it, I Got It!: Conversations with Global Entrepreneurs on Growing Your Audience, Visibility & Influence, and Today's History Makers: 21st Century African American Female Entrepreneurs.*

She has been featured on OWN television network, Essence Magazine, Huffington Post, The Today Show, Tom Joyner Morning Show, TEDx, Johns Hopkins University, NAACP, Congressional Black Caucus, Blacks in Government, FBI, EPA, Good Morning Washington, Great Day Washington, and more.

Tanya has a BS in Social Science. She is currently a MA candidate in Women's Gender and Sexuality Studies at George Washington University in Washington, DC. She is a two-time triathlete and two-time marathoner. She loves historical fiction and hiking with her husband. Tanya is a wife, mom of three young adults, and an energetic Gen-X grandmother.

Contact Tanya Barnett at:
Social Media:
TW - @MsTanyaBarnett1
Website:
https://linktr.ee/tanyabarnett

Foreword

W e are at a critical time in modern history. Nannie Helen Burroughs eloquently stated, "Nobody in the world ever wins success or a place of usefulness until he or she is absolutely wedded to a cause." Helping my fellow human beings during this turbulent time is my passion and the cause I am wedded to.

In advocacy, there are no big "I's or Little You's", no "Us's or Them's". What the world needs, now more than ever, are experienced women like you and I, who are on the front lines actively advocating for those who cannot advocate for themselves. We have to fight for our collective humanity and human rights. We need to come together to ensure everyone's rights are respected regardless of their background, class, gender, ethnicity, ability, national origin, religion, gender expression, gender identity, or sexual orientation. We must be the foot soldiers who enact social justice for our sisters and brothers in crisis.

But how do we do this when the very liberties we hold dear are daily attacked via our racist legal, social, and school systems? We can only accomplish this by providing much-needed services to others. This is our call to action. Contributing to the betterment of our neighbors and empowering our communities is nothing new to women like us. I would dare say, this call to serve runs through our veins.

Today, we confidently open nonprofits where we see a need. Nevertheless, we would do a grave injustice if we did not acknowledge that we stand on the shoulders of women who put their lives on the line for others, especially during slavery. They may not have known that what they were doing was philanthropic yet these sisters recognized their people and they had something, no matter how small, that could fill that void.

The first all-female anti-slavery organization was established in Salem Massachusetts in 1832 and called the *Female Anti-Slavery Society of Salem*. This groundbreaking group was made up entirely of African American women (Burin, 2006). These women held secret meetings under the guise of sewing circles to discuss how to assist those who were in captivity. They also raised funds to assist individuals who had escaped the bonds of slavery. Even though they were privileged and free, they saw it not as robbery to pull their resources together to afford the basic necessities to the newly freed.

Between 1837 and 1847, it was found in Pennsylvania that free Blacks had formed more than eighty benevolent societies for mutual aid in times of sickness and distress. Those voluntary associations were praised for preventing widespread crime and pauperism (Harris, 1979). These societies were birthed by individuals who saw a need. They formed partnerships to ensure their mission was accomplished. These brave Black women knew that they could be jailed or worse but the benefit of helping "the least of these" outweighed the risk of being caught.

There are a myriad of women, whose names we will never know, who gave much so that others may have. Because of the society they lived in, they realized no one was coming to save them and they had to do it themselves. Their sacrifices of time, money, and resources changed lives. I daresay, we may have possibly benefited from their sacrifices in the 21st century.

Jesus states in Matthew 26:11, "You will always have the poor among you." So it goes without saying that we must pick up that mantle and serve those who are still in need. For centuries women have been giving to their neighbors, taking folks in, raising other people's children, and the like. Many of these women gave all they had with the hopes that the people they lent a hand to would have a better life. We have them to thank for providing the blueprint for improving our communities.

Oseola McCarty gave away a life savings of $150,000 to help complete strangers get a college education at the University of Southern Mississippi. She made her small fortune by saving a dollar or two at a time by taking in laundry and ironing. Leah Chase made Dooky Chase's, a Creole restaurant in Louisiana, a meeting place for people like the Freedom Riders of the 1960s. She hosted civil rights meetings in her restaurant which included black voter registration, NAACP meetings, and other political gatherings. Disney's Princess Tiana is loosely based on her.

In 1969, Mother Clara Hale, founded The Hale House, an orphanage for babies. She became a national icon for taking in AIDS-infected, drug-addicted newborns and nurturing them in her home in Harlem. I learned about her when I was in high school and was so moved by her charity that I wrote a report on her in the tenth grade.

Mother Hale's work stuck with me so much so that I begged my parents to become foster parents. Because they felt my passion, they obliged. They fostered an innumerable amount of children for ten years. We had infants through teenagers. I was shocked to hear about the types of households and the abuse these children experienced prior to coming to live with us. When those children left my parents' home, they kept in contact with us. My parents would visit the ones whose parents allowed them to. When I was in the military, I became a foster parent of a crack baby and it was the most humbling experience ever and one I'll never forget.

In the spirit of supporting women businesses and nonprofits, I have volunteered my skills and knowledge to ensure their calling was fulfilled. I understand the value of collective work and the support required to get the job done. I value the struggle of fundraising and putting my own money in other women's vision.

In 2014, I founded Forever Free Books after witnessing a classroom of first-graders who could not read nor owned books. I struggled to teach my students the basics of phonics and felt the burden to alleviate the lack of familial support that most of them lived with. Forever Free Books' goal was to reduce the 3-million-word deficit experienced by low-income children. The distinction was clear, their middle class and wealthy counterparts had access to books which increased exposure to words and increased their vocabulary, thereby, preparing them for school and academic success.

We worked tirelessly to increase literacy for these children by delivering free books to their communities. Because we value partnerships, we worked with other nonprofits, elected officials, and NFL football players. We were empowered to serve these marginalized families by exposing them to college-educated people. Unfortunately, we dissolved in 2020 due to my experiencing a stroke. We were devastated at our closure, but we are determined to continue to provide literacy education when I recover fully. We hail from a community of women who love via service and nothing, including a stroke, can stop us from doing so.

Not only is the need for increasing with COVID-19, the number of people who have immediate and sometimes dire needs are increasing exponentially. This is why "For many are called, but few are chosen" in Matthew 22:14 resonates with me. We can positively impact our neighbors in need now. We've been gifted with the knowledge and the wherewithal to lift them up and to give them the courage to hang on another day. We should honor our ancestors for passing down that gift.

This gift has also been passed on to you from the authors of this compilation. Together we can learn from their fears, disappointments, accomplishments, and their victories. We will follow them along their journey of awareness of a need through the execution of the required steps to achieve their goals. The nonprofit founders in this compilation are exemplary in their craft. They provide us with the indispensable encouragement to fight for the greater good of our fellow citizens.

When you feel weak or imposter syndrome rears its ugly head, please remember, you were chosen for such a time as this. The amount of resources that are available to support you in your nonprofit endeavors is expansive so use them. The authors empower you with unique experiences and through examples of their dedication. All it takes is your willingness and commitment to be the beacon of hope in someone's life.

I love Dr. Maya Angelou's quote, *"Be A Rainbow in Somebody Else's Cloud".* This is the charge we follow as nonprofit founders. Even though we are experiencing cloudy times, your rainbow may be the very thing that saves lives and impacts generations to come. I applaud you for having the courage to adhere to Dr. Angelou's infamous words. May the work of your hands and the sweat of your brow out live you and change the world one life at a time.

Your sister in service,

Tanya Barnett
President of Forever Free Books Nonprofit

Harris, R. (1979). Early Black Benevolent Societies, 1780-1830. The Massachusetts Review, 20(3), 603-625. Retrieved September 7, 2020, from http://www.jstor.org/stable/25088988

Lindhorst, M. (1998). Politics in a Box: Sarah Mapps Douglass and the Female Literary Association, 1831-1833. Pennsylvania History: A Journal of Mid-Atlantic Studies, 65(3), 263-278. Retrieved September 7, 2020, from http://www.jstor.org/stable/27774117

Salerno, Beth A. 2005. Sister Societies: Women's Antislavery Organizations in Antebellum America. DeKalb: Northern Illinois University Press

Introduction

Welcome, Future and Current Legacy Leaders!

I decided to write this book because I wish I had access to nonprofit leaders who shared their experiences with me before and during the beginning stages of my journey in starting my nonprofit. This book, *Nonprofit Legacy,* was birthed because I was truly struggling during this COVID season trying to discover how to ensure that not only my for-profit business, but my nonprofit as well, would survive. God said, let's do something a little different now that you have some time. Let's support others by allowing nonprofit leaders to share their stories. Following God's guidance, I embraced the idea. I wanted leaders in the nonprofit sector to see the power in their stories and their impact so others can learn from their successes and their failures. I interviewed numerous leaders for this compilation; selecting those stories that aligned with my goals for this project. These had to be stories that people could lean on to get them out of a bad situation and give others hope that- "They Can". Nonprofit leaders are so busy in the village doing the work that most don't get to share their stories. Sometimes, not even the people they serve know the journey the leaders have traveled to establish the nonprofit. This is because the leaders' hearts are truly for the cause. I thought as we had an opportunity to be *still* during COVID; we could create something that would inspire current leaders to keep going and ignite future leaders to pick up from where we left off.

My hope is that you as a current leader or a future leader take away the benefits of balancing heart work and head work. You have been led to this work because of your heart; however, I want you to take away from each of these stories that knowledge is power and you need it to sustain your nonprofit. The nonprofits must be sustained for the people you serve. I want you to be encouraged and inspired; to become equipped with tools, and know that you are resilient. I hope this will provide leaders with profound insight and opportunity to take a stance. Leaders can decide-

"To Stay And Continue the Work" or "To Walk Away" or "To Start the Work: If Not Me, Then Who?" The greatest takeaway from all of this is that you are not alone. We are all in this together and when you collaborate everyone wins.

This is the first book that will give you access to both material resources and human resources. For, all of the authors that contributed to this book and their nonprofit organizations are committed to continuing to learn and grow by supporting you in your journey. You will see that there are organizations that you can become a part of and learn from before starting your own. You will also find that you may not have to create an entire organization of your own; there may be an organization out there that needs you to be on their team to provide support in creating and maximizing impact. In the back of the book, there is a directory of all the nonprofits involved in the compilation as well as business owners that will be able to provide guidance and advice so you can start towards building a successful blueprint for your vision for your organization.

However, I want you to remember that obtaining a 501(c)3 does not dictate the success of your organization. What determines success is commitment and reputable resources as well as hard work, dedication, and being honest about the fact that you can't be successful on your own. This compilation is an example of leaders willing to come together to be authentic and very transparent in what it takes to overcome obstacles. They will be the first to tell you that it's not easy. We just want to bless you and your organization with our stories and support you along the way.

"Enjoy The Journey" a quote from one of our co-authors, Sharon Anderson.

~*Author & Visionary Tajala Battle-Lockhart*

Author Allison Bryant

Author Allison Bryant

Allison Bryant is President and Founder of *Tilted Crowns, Inc.*, a nonprofit organization inspiring women and girls. In her role, Allison leads the mentorship organization, now in its fourth year of service. She is a mentor for teens and women alike. Her passion is helping women realize their worth and reminding them to *Rock Their Royalty*.

Allison is an award-winning motivational speaker who enjoys interacting and engaging the audience in conversations, using her wit and class. She is also a two-time award-winning Mentor and Non-Profit Executive.

Managing *Tilted Crowns* virtually has been the highlight of Allison's career. Allison leads the organization's objective of boosting girls from under-resourced communities to fulfill their potential. Under her direction, *Titled Crowns* works with girls in various programs on becoming confident, college-bound, career-focused, and ready to join the next generation of professional women.

Allison has an Associate degree in Business and Leadership, a Bachelor of Science degree in Business Administration, and a Master's degree in Human Development & Family Studies. She is a mother of three beautiful children and she is a grandmother.

Creating a Royalty Mindset

I became more and more filled with pride as I called their names. One by one, I announced the awards, followed by the description of what was required to receive each award and finally the winner's name. I revealed the name of the young person who had earned the award that required a vast amount of work, dedication, and effort. The smiles on the winners' faces were priceless. You see: they had joined a non-profit mentor program for youth named- *Tilted Crowns*. The program took young ladies in on a princess level and nurtured them, built up their self-esteem, introduced them to the concept of self- worth, and taught them that they are *royalty* no matter what they may go through. The girls had to earn the right to cross over in a formal ceremony that was created and centered around them. They had to earn the right to be labeled a *Queen*. It was only fair that I helped them achieve the goal and showed them what it meant to become a queen. I have always believed in showing people how they should be treated. However, I also knew that they had to believe that they were worthy of being treated well.

For an entire school year, the girls would meet and work on different topics and goals that we chose as a group. They had no idea that many of the topics that we worked on as a group were helping me to heal old wounds that I had forgotten even existed. I saw myself in each of these girls and that made it so much easier to help them walk in their greatness. I was raised mainly by my grandmother in the 70's, in Brooklyn New York. My mom was in the picture, but just like many kids, it was my grandma who instilled in me the importance of being morally and ethically sound. She taught me the importance of being someone that I could look in the mirror and be proud of, no matter what others thought of me. My grandmother was a source of stability. However, there came a point when my life was turned upside down. My mother met and married a man in North Carolina and I was forced to leave my grandmother and move to North Carolina with her. That was the first time that I experienced abandonment and hurt on a level that seemed unbearable. "How? Why? How dare you!!" Another traumatic experience was when my grandmother became ill with cancer. My mom and I flew to New York to see her. My grandmother had serious talks with me and gave me a rundown on life and love. She also told me that she would always be near me, even if I didn't see her physically. I didn't understand what my grandmother meant at the time because I was just 13. The very next day my mom told me my grandmother had died. I was in shock! "WAIT!! WHAT? WHY? HOW? WHO DID IT? WHAT ABOUT THIS GOD PERSON THAT Y'ALL CLAIM ANSWERS PRAYERS? WHERE THE HELL IS HE??? You know what... I will ask him myself why he allowed her to die!!" My family is not the type to deal with complex emotional issues, so I had to learn on my own how to deal with the pain of losing my lifeline. I was 13 years old and bitter and angry with this God person because I had cursed him out and he didn't say anything in response. At the same time, I was experiencing adolescence; my body was maturing and developing. I started receiving attention from boys that used to pick at me because I wore the thickest glasses ever created. "Wait. So you don't think I look like a frog anymore? Huh? You have always liked me? Of course, you can kiss me. Wait what is this feeling? Yes, I wanna be your girlfriend; so if I let you do that I will be your girlfriend? I started seeking love in all the wrong places. I was now in search of the feeling of love that I lost when my grandmother died. I searched for years and never found it. I did find out the power of my *womanly wisdom*. I convinced myself that love was love, and if I couldn't get the kind of love that I wanted, then I would hurt everyone that couldn't take the pain away.

I met a boy named Antonio Williams and things seemed to get better. Guess what!! HE HAD A LARGE FAMILY!! Yessss, Jackpot! He had everything that I didn't have. A loving, strong mother, a praying and strong-minded father, and the best sisters I had ever seen. These people sent him to get me for Sunday dinners, and family trips always included me! I finally had a family after four years of feeling lost and lonely. Well, we got a little too comfortable and along came my first creation: my son Antwon! I became a teen mom during my senior year in high school. I would be lying if I said it was easy. My mother and Antonio's entire family stepped up and gave my son the feeling of family that I never had. I had to thank GOD for allowing me to be in the midst of such amazing people. Just as soon as I started to believe this GOD person does exist, I was slapped with another situation. My son has Autism! "Huh? What is that? So now what do I do?" I had to learn what it was and what it meant, so I could help my baby boy achieve greatness. I didn't even know how to raise a child; so raising a child with a *setback* was a challenge.

Then life happened. I moved on and got into a different relationship with a young man named Jamie. He also came with an amazing family, and he loved my son and treated him as if he was his own. Jamie and I were the best of friends and that was a positive in our relationship. He helped me work through a lot of my craziness and helped me learn from my past. We had a daughter named Jay. I felt I couldn't possibly love anymore or be any happier than I was at that time. I realized that a lot of my friends that had kids didn't have it as easy as I did. I also sensed that some people didn't figure it all out as easy or fast as I did, so I took an interest in helping single mothers. However, I was still young and wasn't really sure how to do it. In fact, I kept trying to figure out my life because it wasn't all peaches and cream. Jamie and I were toxic as a couple but awesome co-parents and friends. No, I was not yet ready to support other single moms.

I struggled as a single mom, so I decided to go back to school so I could get a degree, make more money, and provide a better lifestyle for my children. Guess what I ignored. The absence of love in my life. I realized that I didn't like to be lonely and there was a definite void in my life: what I was used to couldn't be filled by my kids. I was scared to be single. I was scared to be alone. I kept dating people that could not benefit my life. However; they kept me from being single and lonely, so they were allowed to *love* me. The sad part of it all is that I didn't love myself; but if you were in my presence and in my life, you damn sure had to love me or else! The final straw was when my boyfriend at the time went back home to visit his mother and made a baby with his neighbor! I was convinced that love was over and overrated.

I know you are probably shocked at this point, but there is more. My low self-esteem and fear of abandonment not only convinced me to get back with him, but to take the baby in. I introduce to you my third child: my daughter, Kanijah. She is one of my favorite people today. If you meet me in person, I will tell you I have three kids. She got disciplined just like the other two. There was no difference. My relationship with her dad ended: yet my relationship with her is still one of the strongest bonds that exist in my life today. She is actually the President of my non-profit organization.

The ultimate change came when I met my executive business coach, Levar Johnson; he shook my existence. He really woke me up and made me think about life and what I was doing wrong. I have always felt that my happiness had to be tied to other people. I felt I needed to be around people to be happy. Levar told me to start dating myself, spend time alone, no phone or anything. Talking about something difficult to do!! It took me almost three months to achieve one date without my phone. I realized I had a problem that needed to be nurtured immediately. Then the Creator allowed Patricia Crisp, ND to enter my life and my world was changed. Patricia Crisp describes herself as a "Classical Naturopath who specializes in healing." Through her guidance, for the first time, I met Allison S. Bryant!! A STAR WAS BORN!! A light lit up inside of me and for the first time in all of my years of existence, I realized that I had to HEAL!! Yep, that was the key to my positive existence. I had to forgive, grieve the correct way, and heal.

I reluctantly began the healing process: slowly but steadily. I learned to meditate, pray, forgive, and love Allison with a different view of who I am. The more I healed the more I wanted to share this new feeling of love, light, and pure energy with others. Then the idea came to pay it forward; helping teens avoid 30 years of bad decisions like I lived through. I decided to volunteer to become a mentor. I called the Boys and Girls Club. I signed on to become a mentor, but they only wanted me to play games and babysit the kids for an hour or two until their parents picked them up. "Nah, that is not what I wanna do." I looked online to see if I could find a nonprofit or a mentor program that would let me truly mentor and provide support to help young girls. Nope, I couldn't find a program out there. I went to the school system to see if I could volunteer to mentor girls at least two hours a week. They wanted me to do a proposal and then come to the school board meetings and present it and wait for the approval. I felt the process was too complicated. I decided I would just create a program on my own. I prayed and meditated for the Creator to guide me. I was offered a speaking engagement at a teen program in Charlotte, North Carolina. In exchange for my service, the Teen Director would share her curriculum and grant me the opportunity to speak to her

Board of Directors to seek help in getting my program started. I went to the meeting and realized that speaking is my purpose. I also realized that I am good at relating to teenagers. I recorded my conversations with the Board and went back to Raleigh with a vengeance. I took the weekend off from the rest of the world and went to the beach alone. I came back home with the name, vision, mission, and purpose for my mentor program. I formed my board after sharing my vision with some key individuals. They all agreed to come on and assist in any way possible. A great friend of mine did a newspaper article highlighting me and the design and purpose of my program. On the same day, the phone was ringing and emails were popping up faster than I could read them! I had my power crew. I held interviews with each parent and each girl to see if I was a fit for them and if they were a fit for the team. I started with seven girls the first year.

The program was a success. I saw grades go up, attitudes shift, and self-esteem skyrocket. I was so happy to see the girls put forth so much effort to not only change their lives, but to be an influence to each other. I wanted to do something big for them to show them that their hard work and dedication to becoming the best version of themselves to date was worth it. I created the Crowning Ceremony to show the girls that they are worthy of all the praise that comes with being a Queen. During the Crowning Ceremony, each girl had to recite the *Tilted Crowns* creed. Instead of crowns, they were given bracelets with crowns on them and I proclaimed that they were now Queens. They were given awards according to their accomplishments. The final task was for each of them to perform a talent. The girls were so nervous, but the standing ovations they received, produced immediate confidence and pride, as evidenced by the huge smiles on their faces.

The second year I had thirteen girls and a bigger idea of what to do for them. However, life happened and I lost most of my Board. I didn't feel alone. I didn't feel abandoned. I felt motivated to still make the program a success and put the girls in the program to work since it was their program, too. They agreed to hold elections and assign duties to the elected officials of the group. It was an amazing year and I realized the best thing you can do for our youth is equip them for the real world. My focus has shifted to do just that.

If you are reading this because you have a desire to start a non-profit and you don't know where or how to start, my advice to you is to:

- Write out your vision. Be detailed. There is no idea that is too grand or too small. Write out the details and just start somewhere.

- Pray and ask the Creator to put people in your presence who can assist with your vision or can open the doors to your vision.

- Don't worry about the 501c 3 part immediately. Determine what you want to do and how you want to do it. Research and see if there are laws that govern the operation of your specific nonprofit or limitations that must be considered and act accordingly. The fact that you are even considering helping others shows your greatness and for that this Queen salutes you.

Personal Reflections/Notes
Nonprofit Wisdom & Insights

_____

_____

_____

_____

_____

_____

_____

_____

_____

_____

_____

Personal Reflections/Notes
Nonprofit Wisdom & Insights

_____

_____

_____

_____

_____

_____

_____

_____

_____

_____

_____

_____

_____

Author Chemeka Turner-Williams

Author Chemeka Turner-Williams

Dr. Chemeka Turner-Williams is a woman "of many hats" who is PURPOSE DRIVEN. She is one who triumphs in the face of adversity; she overcomes and beats all odds against her. Dr. Williams is a Faith Walker who's not afraid to take risks. She's a woman who gracefully maneuvers through the hardships of life, family, ministry, and business. She's a trailblazer who is lighting the way. She's a mother setting the example and leading the path for her four amazing children: Tatiyanna, Shaleik, Naseyah, and Nacyiah. Her children have pushed her and encouraged her as she completed her God-given assignments to serve others. She is building a foundation for her children to be trailblazers and powerful leaders who will use their God-given gifts to help make a difference in the lives of others and impact their communities globally. Chemeka is the daughter of Angela Faye Turner of Halifax County, North Carolina.

Dr. Chemeka Turner-Williams is the visionary, often described as a "new and unique voice in the earth", delivering entrenched messages of inspiration and empowerment from a fresh perspective. Dr. Williams has utilized her oratorical abilities and scholarship to advocate for many causes. She skillfully infuses motivational and perspicacious teachings with a sense of history and the contributions of modern thinkers and teachers. As a result, Dr. Williams has earned the reputation of being both a dynamic and relevant speaker and educator. Dr. Williams is a Minister serving in the House of Mandate located in Roanoke Rapids, North Carolina. She serves under the tutelage and leadership of her Pastor and Spiritual Father, Dr. Orin Perry. Dr. Williams is a Chief Executive Officer(CEO), Chief Operating Officer (COO), author, social entrepreneur, philanthropist, and seasoned humanitarian. She is recognized as an African American female leader who gets results. She possesses the courage to help change situations for women and children who have been affected by domestic violence and abuse, homelessness, and incarceration. Dr. Williams has a strong commitment to education, the economic empowerment of women, and meaningful leadership. Over the years, Dr. Williams has assisted more than 5000 women and children in crisis through educational programs, and the distribution of food, clothing, and personal care items at no cost to the recipients. In addition, she has single-handedly initiated and coordinated numerous corporate and community outreach programs.

Dr. Williams received her Doctorate of Education in Organizational Leadership & Management from the University of Berkley, in September 2020, her Ed.S (Educational Specialist in School Administration) from Cambridge College in 2013, Masters of Education in Counseling from Cambridge College, and her Bachelors in Elementary Education from North Carolina Central University. Dr. Williams launched Pearls of Purpose Inc, a world-wide feminist organization for women and children of all ages. *PEARLS OF PURPOSE INC.* is a Nonprofit Organization focused on Supporting and Empowering WOMEN and CHILDREN in Crisis. *PEARLS OF PURPOSE INC.* focuses especially on abused women and children, children affected by incarceration, and women and children facing homelessness and human trafficking. This organization provides quality coaching & development through empowerment events, mentorship, healing seminars, and personal coaching sessions.

In 2018, Dr. Williams launched NEXT LEVEL COACHING & CONSULTING LLC, a global business and leadership development consultancy serving the world's top entrepreneurs, CEOs, and business executives by helping them to dramatically grow their businesses, develop their people, and elevate their own performance. Dr. Williams also serves as the Chief Operations Officer of Mandate Enterprise, a rising Fortune 500 company. An educator in public and private schools for 17 years, she also served in various roles throughout her community. Dr. Williams served as the Town Commissioner of Garysburg, North Carolina, overseeing the Parks & Recreation Department for four years. She served on several boards: including the Town of Garysburg Community Development Corporation, the Board of Roanoke Valley Adult Day Center, and the Department of Public Safety (DPS) of the Women's Correctional Institution for several years.

Dr. Williams has a mission to help the lost, and aid the broken-hearted. She's also a licensed and ordained minister who has a passion to see women and young adults excel in their faith, family, business, finances, and healthcare. Filled with the desire to not only share her story of adversity, triumph, and success, Dr. Williams is a woman on the rise, impacting lives globally. She is leading in the community; bringing about change and answers to global issues. As a result of her dedication and commitment to the up-building of people and communities, Dr. Williams was nominated by *ACHI* magazine as the 2018 Community Leader of the Year and the 2019 Philanthropist of the Year. She has also been featured in *Creating Your Seat at the Table* magazine for her entrepreneurial and philanthropist endeavors. Her community efforts and initiatives have impacted communities near and far. She is a three times published author with the release of her latest book, *Surviving in Silence: Overcoming Domestic Violence.* This book is a tool and resource guide to ending this hidden issue that has embedded itself in our society. Dr. Williams will continue to be the salt of the Earth; impacting lives wherever her feet may tread. She is LEADING & OVERCOMING ON PURPOSE!!!

Connect to Dr. Chemeka Turner Williams:

For more information about Speaking engagements, Business and Leadership Coaching packages, Ministry Leadership Trainings, or Domestic Violence Trainings and workshops and events www.chemekaturnerwilliams.com
Email: chemekaturnerwilliams@gmail.com
Facebook: @Chemeka Turner-Williams @pearlsofpurposeinc @nextlevelcoachingandconsultingLLC @msblacknorthcarolina2019 **Instagram:** @Chemeka Turner-Williams

Positioned for Purpose

D o you hear the SILENT SCREAMS? Do you see the SILENT VICTIMS? Do you hear the cries of desperation for help? Who will answer the call to serve those seeking help and a safe place in our communities? Over recent decades, light has been shed on many issues that had previously been often overlooked and ignored in our societies. Some of these issues include domestic violence and abuse, incarceration, and homelessness. Women and children are suffering and enduring daily, yet many turn their heads to the woman or child tattered with bruises and scarred emotionally. Society will walk past those roaming the streets in search of shelter and food. The world will turn a deaf ear to the sound of the pain of the women and children who are mourning the loss of a parent or spouse due to incarceration. Domestic violence has no boundaries or socio-economic, racial, cultural, and class distinctions. This epidemic is not only increasing geographically, but its incidence is also extensive, making it a normal and accepted behavior by our societies. Domestic violence is widespread, deeply knitted in our communities and cultures and has serious impacts on women and children's health and well-being. It is a burden on numerous sectors of the social system and quietly, yet dramatically, affects the development of a nation.

Many affected by domestic violence often experience homelessness as well as mental health issues that stem from abuse. Escaping domestic violence is a huge cause of homelessness for women, youth, and families. Many times the victims of domestic violence are cut off from their support systems, networks, and their finances, leaving them little resources with which to make their escape. Living in fear, many mothers and children bury their faces in their hands, wiping away the sleep and frustration from their eyes. They question if they will survive. Then, we have children with incarcerated parents. These children are a vulnerable population: silent victims who are often overlooked and forgotten. Often, families are ripped apart by incarceration and left with emotional and psychological damage because their loved one is no longer there to provide for and nurture them. Each of these areas has transformed the lives of women and children. Many women and children have found themselves standing alone, with little to no resources, and lack of support for emotional, mental, and financial needs.

I know all too well about domestic violence, homelessness, and families affected by incarceration. I have had to endure and overcome each of these traumas in my very own life. I have worn the scars and bruises as if they were makeup. I endured and suffered domestic violence from the time I was a teenager until I was an adult because I was too fearful and ashamed of what my life had become. I was embarrassed and self-conscious in my own skin; not having anywhere to turn nor a place to seek help. Battered with no safe place to go. Screaming for help, yet no one heard my silent screams. My pillow and Kleenex were saturated with tears because I was "Surviving in Silence". If only my tears and pain could talk!! It seemed as if I was dying mentally, emotionally, physically and spiritually. Someone had entered in and destroyed the very thing that you need to *live*. Later in life, my family was ripped apart when my then spouse was incarcerated. I was blindsided by everything that was happening. This transition was confusing and painful to me, as well as my children. Again, I experienced a loss and a big life change. Immediate impacts included a sense of shame, guilt, social stigmatization, loss of financial support, increased risk of abuse, or neglect. As I looked around, silently suffering from the impact of what had transpired, I knew this was not going to be my end.

As I overcame these obstacles I made a vow that I would always help and support other women and children affected by these issues. I began to research and explore what supports were available. I found out early that resources, programs, and educational components were missing in our communities. The programs and resources that could assist women and children that were facing these life-altering situations were scarce if not hidden. That is how and why the nonprofit, **Pearls of Purpose Inc.** was birthed. **Pearls of Purpose Inc.** is a nonprofit organization created to Empower the Scared, the Silent, and the Abused. This nonprofit organization focuses on Supporting and Empowering WOMEN and CHILDREN in Crisis. The vision is to Educate, Advocate and bring awareness to and prevent abuse of women and children, children affected by incarceration, and mothers facing homelessness. These issues that are heavily present in our communities can have a tremendous impact on children's education, health, sense of safety, and overall development.

Pearls of Purpose Inc. assists women and children in the healing process by changing lives, helping families, and rebuilding communities affected by these dark issues. *Pearls of Purpose Inc.* is committed to implementing a comprehensive plan to prevent domestic violence and child abuse and neglect in all its forms (sexual, physical, mental, and emotional), through programs, safety training, services, public awareness, education, advocacy, networking and mentorship/ coaching programs. In addition, *Pearls of Purpose Inc.* has forged collaborative partnerships with the community, judicial systems, and faith-based organizations. Through these partnerships, the organization has initiated and coordinated numerous corporate and community outreach programs. We are committed to bringing support and resources to survivors across the nation, educating our nation about the effects of domestic violence, homelessness, and ending the misunderstandings and stigma surrounding these issues in our communities. For families affected by incarceration, we have been able to provide behavioral, academic, and empowerment programs for children who have one or both parents in prison. The program also includes creating referrals to community resources and other services that also help families cope with incarceration. These support services have helped affected women and children transform from victims into survivors who have reclaimed their lives and live without violence and fear of further abuse, neglect, and lack of basic needs being met.

Creating and starting a *nonprofit* is so rewarding. You seek to provide an answer to many issues in our communities and the help that so many individuals are in need of. With the rewards, there are many challenges that entrepreneurs face when starting a nonprofit. Those that seek and desire to start up a nonprofit must consider many variables that play in the development of the organization. Many decisions will have to be made on how they wish the organization to function. Some of the challenges are obvious, while others are not so obvious in the startup process. With the birth of new nonprofit organizations, there are all sorts of threats associated with the startup and stability of the organization. I have discovered that private organizations are very vulnerable in their early stages of development. In order to sustain your organization and achieve your mission, you need to be aware of these issues and how they could affect your nonprofit. Some of these issues include capital, understanding of the market, a success model to attract and maintain that market, visibility in the community, and availability of resources. Throughout the process of establishing and the startup of *Pearls of Purpose Inc,* the challenges and opposition seemed overwhelming. Many times I found myself searching and seeking support and none was found. Sometimes in this field, individuals are not as willing as they could be to help others with information that could assist in the development of the nonprofit and ensure success.

My purpose and desire to serve those looking for support and a better way of living was my driving force for *Pearls of Purpose Inc.* As I implemented more community and educational programs to serve those in need, I realized that more structure and support was needed. The development of a capable and committed Board of Directors who had the time to invest in the mission was critical and necessary. I needed an effective board to ensure that the organization's mission is being carried out in the most appropriate way. It's a huge responsibility and it's not to be taken lightly. Like many nonprofit founders have experienced, I discovered it was difficult to decide who will be "right" for the organization. Finding like-minded individuals to take on core leadership responsibilities and the challenges of moving the *Pearls of Purpose Inc.* to the next level was draining and frustrating at many times. I found myself with individuals that had the time but not the expertise or the skill, or individuals who had the skill and expertise but not the time to invest in the vision.

Getting the right Board members and having them to step up to the plate and govern and steer *Pearls of Purpose Inc.* in the direction of the mission seemed unobtainable. It was exhausting and many times was a distraction to completing the main task at hand. Over a period of time, the board finally became cohesive and was diverse in various, important ways. I finally felt that we had the right fit. I was also excited that I had a couple of my closest, loyal friends that I considered to be *family*, who had decided to be a part of the board. I completely trusted them and they had the same mindset as I when it came to business. One of these special friends was appointed board chair. She demonstrated great concern and was thorough in all matters pertaining to taking the organization to another level. We were in the trenches together, following the vision and mission and fighting for the same cause. Things were looking up. *Pearls of*

Purpose Inc. was continuing to grow and expand with the guidance of the Board. But too often when people are too close to us, we ignore the obvious, which can be costly. I was beginning to learn a hard lesson; sometimes friends are wolves in sheep's clothing. My chair was having private conversations with integral partners and key stakeholders that were contrary to the vision. This individual would disclose sensitive information; this was a definite conflict of interest. These were signs of disloyalty, mistrust, and possible sabotage. Needless to say, the one I trusted with the vision and mission of the organization was quickly causing damage to the organization. Tension was building, interpersonal conflicts were escalating, difficulties related to how decisions were made, and by whom started coming to the forefront. She was driven by her own personal motives. These behaviors were toxic to the organization. There were so many emotions and feelings because of who the individual was to me. I had to think of the best interest of the organization and the people we serve. When an individual starts to interfere with your board's work and hinders progress, it's time to take action. The board did address the issues and behaviors that were presented which led to the implementation of more structural mechanisms, training and staff development, defining clear roles and responsibilities, and more productive engagement of the board. It was deemed necessary that a revamping of the board would take place. Regardless of what challenges come up I never lost sight of the purpose of what we are called to do. *Pearls of Purpose Inc.'s* commitment to empowering women and children and thereby strengthening families and transforming communities was the driving force. We continued to improve on our weakness and moved forward for the greater cause. Our service to the women, children and families of our communities was our priority.

Another major challenge that I encountered along this journey of developing a nonprofit was finding the money to accomplish the mission and goals of *Pearls of Purpose Inc.* Funding is imperative to keep our doors open. For several years, I personally funded all the daily operations, functions, events, trainings, and community initiatives. *Pearls of Purpose Inc.* was conducting quarterly distributions of meal packages, and winter clothing and blankets to the homeless. We prepared meals for over 1,000 domestic violence victims yearly, we provided clothing to disadvantaged youth, as well as to various shelters throughout the state. We provided academic support and tutoring sessions and mentored the youth impacted by domestic violence and incarceration. Most of the finances were provided personally or from family and friends who believed in the mission and vision of the organization. Therefore, there was limited funding available to assist with the cause. In our beginning stages we were able to capitalize on various in-kind gifts, such as free service space, use of free equipment, and other non-financial donations from local businesses and professionals. This was a great way to offset some of the financial needs.

It became clear that I needed help in seeking funding, fundraisers, donors, and sponsors for the mission and goals of the organization. It was definitely a difficult process, not knowing where to go next. It became evident that the smaller nonprofits had to compete with the larger, more established nonprofits to get the attention of donors. Even though it was challenging, we started focusing on marketing and investing more time in social media or community events, trying to become more visible to investors. We were getting the organization visible and we decided to partner up with other organizations and community leaders in our area and feed off each other's strengths and resources. Connecting with similar nonprofits to pool resources was believed to be beneficial. There were nonprofits that had essentially the same mission with the same basic objectives. We quickly realized that we were missing critical components: networking and building relationships. That was the next step, collaboration and networking at an advanced level. Through collaboration and partnering with other organizations, government agencies, and community events, we gained better insights and strategic ideas. We were able to accomplish more at a lower overall cost; it kept us from making our load heavier. Partnering with each nonprofit or organization had its own unique sphere of influence and combined together we expanded the ability to advance our shared goals and our individual missions. Through the new partnerships and relationships formed, *Pearls of Purpose Inc.* was getting attention across various sectors and gaining knowledge of many funding opportunities and resources.

Nonprofit organizations of any kind have a very crucial responsibility and role in building healthy communities. *Pearls of Purpose Inc.* is dedicated to serving women, children, families, and communities despite the challenges that have been encountered and those we may encounter in the future. We are committed to further its mission by meeting the safety needs of victims, while also participating in transformative change that will better equip our community to respond to domestic violence, homelessness, and strive to end this public health epidemic. Even though starting and sustaining a nonprofit can be a challenging task, it is rewarding and beneficial to those we are committed to helping. I encourage each leader that has the desire to take the journey into establishing a nonprofit to do their homework: research and conduct a needs analysis. See if there are other organizations doing similar work in the area. Build a solid foundation from the inside out. You want to make sure you have established the mission and purpose of what you are doing, as well as who you are called to serve and how you will serve them. When developing your board, be strategic in the selection process. You want to ensure that you include orientation, provide proper training and evaluation to build long term success. The success of nonprofits is in the building of relationships and building trust with partners and networks. Lastly, apply for your 501(c)(3) status. You will also need your board to be supportive in locating other funds and resources to sustain the nonprofit. The board must understand that the nonprofit is sustained through fundraising.

Never give up on the people we are called to serve. Transform your vision and passion into purpose. The work that we do is making an everlasting impact in communities across the world. You are the answer someone is looking for.

Personal Reflections/Notes
Nonprofit Wisdom & Insights

Author Dee Sapp

Author Dee Sapp

Dee Sapp has over 13 years of nonprofit administrative, front-line fundraising, program management, and managerial experience. She's served on several boards at both the community and state levels; most to advocate and support people with disabilities.

Currently, Dee serves on The Maryland Developmental Disabilities Council where members are appointed by the Governor to establish the priorities of the Council and help guide the Council's work. She also serves as an accessibility editor for the Maryland State Arts Council.

Dee has a son with autism and an intellectual disability and she feels strongly that all children should learn, play, and advance in inclusive environments. She supports her son, a US Paralympic Team member and swimmer, to advocate for himself and focuses on advocacy for people who are differently-abled and their families. She's a graduate of the Southern MD LEADers program and is active in a variety of committees. Dee aspires to be part of a national systems transformation and propagate consciousness about inclusive practices so that all facets of community life – school, work, social activities – welcome people with developmental disabilities.

Dee is the founder and CEO of The Accessibility Bridge Corporation, a 501 (c) (3) nonprofit corporation that encourages differently-abled people to integrate into a larger society and connects them with resources and communities that will make this integration as seamless as possible. Dee's most recent professional experiences include nine years at Georgetown University in the Office of Advancement and two years at Catholic Charities as a Major Gift Officer.

Dee's institutions of higher learning include North Carolina State University (Business Management), Georgetown University (Liberal Studies), and Penn State University (Human Development and Family Studies with a concentration in Life Span Human Services). Dee is a married mother of three children and a native of Charlotte, NC but has raised her family in Southern Maryland and made it her home for the last 18 years.

Accessibility Bridge Corporation, Chief Executive Officer
WEBSITE: https://accessibilitybridge.com/
FACEBOOK: facebook.com/accessbridge/ TWITTER: twitter.com/accessbridgesco

Inclusion Matters

I'm affectionately coined as "the lady with the words". I use specific language to communicate my thoughts and I make every effort to convey words in manners that are unambiguous, concise, and appropriate. It would be highly admirable to say that my communication style is due to years of formal educational training, but it instead stemmed from 18 years of "sink or swim", on-the-job training as the mother of a child with autism and an intellectual disability (ID). I'm not sharing this information with you in an effort to invite pity or imply burden. I share only to provide context to my journey and hopefully deliver an interminable story of resilience and hope.

My son is the type of person that has never adapted to or accepted the "can't do" mentality. Telling him that he can't do something will guarantee that he's going to try harder until he's overcome a challenge, and then swiftly move to his next objective. He provides inspiration as well as the feelings associated with a thrilling, yet exhausting rollercoaster ride. He's always been around children his age and I've never exclusively socialized him with people that had diagnosed impairments. He wanted to play soccer, so I enrolled him in a soccer program. He wanted to swim, so I enrolled him in a swim program. No apology or explanation given; he's a child that wants to play, so let him play. As a young child, he was treated like any other kid by coaches and teachers, which is exactly how things should've been. As he got older, I learned that this unconditional acceptance was the exception, not the standard.

Once he reached middle school, some of his teachers weren't as engaged as teachers from his elementary school. I chalked it up to them preparing him for high school and giving students more responsibility and accountability. As time went on, I also noticed that I was informed less of his progress and setbacks outside of the Individualized Educational Plan (IEP) meetings and responses to my questions were met with either avoidance or agitation. I realized that other people recognized that my son was "extraordinary", but not in the same way that I saw him. I regarded him as someone with attributes of a person with Intellectual Disability (ID); yet one who defies stereotypes and preconceived limits and can push past boundaries with good-hearted assistance. Some teachers treated him like a disabled child that needed to learn to follow the system that ostensibly worked for so many "like" him and saw his desire for independence and inclusion as problematic and defiant.

High school was an intensified version of this same systemic bottleneck. His school had predetermined boxes and checklists and only wanted to decide which of their boxes he gets placed in and which items could be checked off their list. A different school would have yielded different sets of boxes and potentially different checklists. So at times, it could be deduced that the success of a person with a disability is based on the luck of the draw; non-strategic and nonspecific. I sometimes met their nicely packaged box presentation with rejection because it felt like we were discussing someone else's child in most of his IEP meetings. There's an indescribable type of hurt that's felt when the people who are employed to look out for the best interest of your child, sit in silence when they see an injustice being served by their colleagues and cower when the opportunity to speak up or take action arrives. Their silence was deafening and still speaks volumes as I share this with you today. Ultimately, I decided to remove him from the public school system and focus on what was best for him and not entertain what was easiest and cheapest for the decision-makers and their staff.

Apart from his tiresome academic journey, he's an amazing athlete who has been competing as a national team member on the United States Paralympic Swim team. He is also a freshman at a four-year University that is over eight hours away from our home. We're living during a time when words like "diversity" and "inclusion" are used to launch impactful initiatives within large organizations and smaller groups. Some people and organizations use these words to exude the appearance of diversity and inclusion just so they're staying with the current trends, but their actions and willingness to do a deep dive into what diversity and inclusion really look like illustrates otherwise. It's uncommon for people with autism and ID to be athletically gifted, but it does happen - my son is proof of that. We were fortunate to find a USA Swimming team located about 30 minutes from our home that welcomed him and his disability with open arms. He was one of the first differently-abled, talented swimmers that came through that location, but the coaches, parents, and teammates chose to recognize and respect his potential rather than focus on his deficiencies. I've come to understand that the culture of this swim club was another exception, not the rule. Customarily, the rules that schools, organizations, and communities employ to establish and maintain order, are exclusionary in nature (whether intended or not) and leave people like my son sitting in deep gaps with no viable opportunities for inclusion or employable development. A few months ago, I connected with the mom of a boy that my son previously attended school with. Her son also had an IEP. She asked me what my son's plans were after high school and when I told her that he was going to college, she mentioned that she didn't know what her son was going to do. She admitted that dealing with the school system and getting her son to the point where he finally graduated was so arduous that she feels that she's finally given up the fight. She also remarked that I'm the type of mother that children like our sons need to make them successful. My conversation with this fatigued, yet courageous mom made my heart sorrowful, but also gave me the endorsement I needed to keep pressing onward. I'm no longer in this battle only for my son, but for all the differently-abled people that have either fallen or been shoved in the gaps of our educational, governmental, or social systems. Guiding my son while he overcame obstacles is confirmation that placing people in metaphorical boxes hinders their ability to grow, isolates them, and isn't how you show value to people who want to be active and contributing members of our society.

The end of the first phase of my son's journey inspired the commencement of my nonprofit organization, *The Accessibility Bridge Corporation.* Ruminating on my adverse encounters while attending IEP meetings and engaging with leaders in our public-school community continues to give me the fuel needed to drive my cause forward. There's strength in the wake of our traumas and our roots are integral parts of our foundation. An unintended benefit of the negative experiences my son endured is that they helped me find the voice I needed to better serve those who aren't able to accurately articulate their wants or needs. Differently-abled people have human rights and want to live dignified, independent lives and aren't always in positions to either defend or advocate for these rights. Social systems play vital roles in who we are as humans and inclusion matters. There are communities around the world that are inclusive of differently-abled people and don't provoke conflict when a person is requesting equal opportunities or equitable solutions. The goal of *The Accessibility Bridge Corporation* is to inform differently-abled people, their caregivers, and families that there's hope and opportunity waiting for them in communities outside of their own. Our organization aspires toward inclusive excellence, nurturing professional relationships, obtaining resources, creating inclusive communities, and making differently-abled people aware of inclusive opportunities.

As a nonprofit executive, there are principles that I needed to mentally reconcile in successfully launching a corporation that would eventually self-sustain and continue to fulfill its timeless mission. The first of these principles is to be unafraid to walk alone. For several years, I'd been throwing around the idea of starting a nonprofit to help differently-abled people. I didn't know how I'd do it or what it would look like, so I was exploring the idea of collaborating with other businesses or working with other people. I thought that if I had assistance building my nonprofit, it would have a stronger foundation and give me time to cautiously proceed with this venture. I discovered that being a successful nonprofit leader requires a mission-focused mindset that not everyone who says they want to help you may have. There are occasions when the weight of your mission is exceptionally heavy and there's no one else willing or capable to assist in carrying the responsibility. I've learned to manage this "weight" by not seeing it as burdensome, but as a part of the purpose that I've been tasked to achieve. This is my mission; therefore, it's my work. Willingly doing any of the duties required to implement and advance the mission allows employees and volunteers to see how committed I am to this cause. A manager who's complicit in allowing others to do more for the organization than they're prepared to do demonstrates the qualities of a boss, not a leader. A leader inspires with their behind-the-scenes behaviors, not by their words or the person they portray to be on paper or on social media.

I next learned to surround myself with like-minded people. There are countless nonprofits, both large and small, but not all nonprofits' organizations are equal. Not all nonprofits have founders who remain committed to their primary vision and stay true to their mission. Some take the minimalist approach by doing the least amount of work and expecting to derive benefits equal to those founders who invest large amounts of sweat equity into keeping their organizations growing, thriving, and authentic. It's difficult to see what a person truly believes if you haven't seen their sacrifices. The ultimate test of integrity is what people are willing to risk to maintain their core values. In co-authoring this book, I've engaged with other authors and understand what inspired their entrepreneurship, what has kept them motivated, and how they keep their nonprofits flourishing. While our leadership characteristics and goals may differ, the hunger and desire for success and service are similar in many ways. Some of the other authors (also nonprofit leaders) are humble, creative, resourceful, impactful, global, inspirational, encouraging, authentic, passionate, and skilled. There's much to give and much to learn when you're surrounded by people who are on the same path you're on. Inevitably, our paths will split, but appreciating the camaraderie and knowledge while being merged on this journey presents advantages to each of us. Discovering how to identify the sheep from the shepherds is paramount. Shepherds lead by charting the way for their entire flock while sheep are only interested in where they want to go and what's in their immediate interest. I hesitantly, but necessarily dissociated myself from people who had motives and intentions contradictory to my own. I established a more productive group of mentors and partners based on shared values, commitments, and sincerities. I have an amazing board of advisors with years of vetted experience in their fields, proven successes and desires to not only help *The Accessibility Bridge Corporation* grow, but to keep me accountable while offering their expert and personal advice. I have an executive committee that's willing to step in and assist wherever and however they are needed. They help build and promote our programs which in turn helps propel the mission and the vision of *The Accessibility Bridge Corporation* forward. The value that my board of advisors and executive committee members bring to the organization is immeasurable and I'd be remiss if I didn't acknowledge their contributions.

Lastly, you must engage with the population that you provide for. It's one thing to sell a concept or idea to donors in efforts to obtain dollars to help your organization. However, it's another thing to interact with the constituents you're raising money to benefit. Understanding both the basic and complicated needs of the people you serve and support is critical in the success of your advocacy and fundraising efforts. Living, engaging with, and advocating for my son has given me almost 19 years of hands-on experience and understanding of the intricate details of living and working with someone with autism and an intellectual impairment. While on my journey with him, I've been fortunate to meet others who have different impairments than his and learn about their journeys, what they want, what they need, and how I can help them achieve their goals. Even though I'm responsible for the work of **The Accessibility Bridge Corporation** at the executive level, I still make it a part of my duties to be engaged in the work at the grassroots and service levels.

The journey of a nonprofit leader can be exhausting, but it also reaps an incalculable amount of rewards. It's astonishing the number of alliances that are cultivated along the way, the new connections with old acquaintances and former colleagues, and the warm emotions that come from doing a job well by providing for and encouraging others. When you're enthusiastic about the cause that you endorse, it doesn't feel like work at all. You'll do the work by going the extra mile, extending your comfort zone, thinking creatively and strategically to see your vision come to fruition. If you're not ready to launch or lead a nonprofit, I encourage you to either work for or volunteer for an organization that closely meets your interests. There's much to learn about how nonprofits operate, but there is also much to learn about what our world needs and the people that go above and beyond what's expected of them to assist those in need. Being a part of something that is much bigger than you gives you added purpose and will hopefully inspire you to do more for others without expecting anything tangible in return. The recipe for nonprofit success is simple – always uphold your commitment to service and maintain your desire to learn and develop.

My son is still very independent-minded which is what I'd think our society would prefer over someone who always looks to others for help or assistance. I envision a world where people are free to move about without fear of discrimination, retaliation, or inequity. My vision is not due to naivety, but due to hope. There is no remedy for human nature and I alone am not able to solve or fight for all the world's injustices. I will give my best and do my part by continuing to push for inclusive education, inclusive workplaces, inclusive communities, and most importantly an inclusive mindset. Inclusion works and inclusion matters.

Personal Reflections/Notes
Nonprofit Wisdom & Insights

Personal Reflections/Notes
Nonprofit Wisdom & Insights

Author Erica Perry Green

Author Erica Perry Green

Erica Perry Green is a woman who has risen against great odds to find her *God-given Purpose!* With an intense passion and desire to see everyone win, Erica focused her career on leading, coaching, and mentoring sales professionals in the corporate space. Erica has held managerial and executive level positions in both pharmaceutical companies and educational firms. Managing multi-million dollar accounts and sales professionals across six states, Erica currently serves as a Regional Executive Director of Healthcare. Erica has focused her twenty-year career in sales, marketing, and training.

While rising through the ranks in Corporate America, Erica had a strong desire to own her own business and create a legacy that would out-live her. For the last six years, Erica has been successful in various business and marketing endeavors; including launching SHERO Publishing Company, focused on helping women to Unleash their inner SHERO and share their stories with the world. Erica is also a three-time author herself; publishing her book, *Unleash Your SHERO* and sharing her literary work as a best-selling co-author in *A Reason to Be, Love Pack* and *Wake, Pray, Slay.* Erica also founded Green Business Consulting Firm, supporting entrepreneurs to grow, scale, and market their business. Erica serves as an ICF Certified Business & Life Coach, supporting business owners to maximize their success.

As a skilled entrepreneur, Erica has traveled the world, training and assisting new business owners in growing and developing their brand. Erica is passionate about mentoring and coaching entrepreneurs on the concept of multiple streams of income. Erica has also ascended to top ranks in two global businesses; creating networks of thousands of business partners. As a master sales trainer and marketer, Erica is also partnered with Einnaf Cosmetics, serving as their Global Sales & Marketing Director for the entire Ambassador Sales Team; expanding the company globally.

Giving back has always been at Erica's core. For the last ten years, Erica served in pivotal roles in several nonprofits, all supporting women and youth. While serving as a Historian for WINGS Women's Group, Erica led numerous mission and community endeavors, including a trip to support village development in the Dominican Republic. Erica also served as a part of Solo Mom Foundation, supporting single mothers in local Raleigh/Durham shelters.

Throughout all of her outreach efforts, Erica had a strong desire to give back in an even more impactful way. With an intense passion for lifting and supporting those in need, Erica founded *Sisters Lifting Sisters*, a 501C3 nonprofit organization focused on supporting women and children at risk. *Sisters Lifting Sisters* supports women facing hunger issues & homelessness, single mothers, domestic violence survivors, and women facing health issues. To date, SLS Nonprofit has supported over 6,000 women and children through annual food and clothing pantries, GIRLS 2 WOMEN Empowerment events, backpack drives and hosting an annual Christmas brunch and gift giveback for women and their families in residential rehabilitation facilities in Wake and Orange County. Erica has received numerous awards for her philanthropy and community services, including the 2018 ACHI Nonprofit Leader of the Year Award.

Throughout all of her philanthropic endeavors, family remains first! Erica enjoys traveling the world and spending time with her loving husband and best friend of twenty-three years, Jonathan Green, and daughter, Camryn. Following in her mother's footsteps, Camryn became a CEO at the age of 8. She is now a junior in high school. Erica works hard to ensure that Camryn is raised, understanding that she must utilize her gifts and talents to empower others and above all else, serve her community. She truly is one of Erica's *SHEROS!*

Connect with Erica Perry Green:
Business Coaching: ericaperrygreen.com
Publishing: sheropublishing.com
Facebook: @ericaperrygreen
Instagram: @ericapgreen
ericaperrygreen@gmail.com
(919) 522-8195

Unleashing Their SHERO!

I have an intense passion to support women! For over 12 years I have worked and served with three different women-focused nonprofits: all supporting and empowering women fighting homelessness, drug abuse, and domestic violence. I spent hours sitting with these women, listening to their stories, and being just as inspired and empowered from them as I pray they were from me. I can recall carving time out of my work schedule to head to downtown Raleigh to unmarked buildings to volunteer at homeless shelters, serving lunch, providing canned goods and clothing donations. I spent a lot of time meeting with center directors and finding out their needs.

So many women in centers and shelters leave their homes in such an emergency situation that they arrive without clothing or toiletries. I started campaigns to stock pile centers with welcome kits for women, so that no woman, fleeing a domestic situation, had to worry about having a toothbrush or toothpaste. These women gave me strength.

Through my work, volunteering and intense passion for giving back, I decided to take my service to the next level by founding *Sisters Lifting Sisters*, a nonprofit. *Sisters Lifting Sisters* or SLS is a 501C3 focused on empowering women and children by bridging the gap between those who need assistance and available local resources. SLS serves **WOMEN AT RISK,** including single mothers facing homelessness, hunger, domestic violence, and women facing health issues.

SLS is partnered with UNC Horizon and several local inpatient rehabilitation centers and women's shelters to provide monthly support to residents and women in need. SLS also provides collaborative resources to women and children, including connecting women facing homelessness or women fleeing domestic environments with the resources, support and tools needed for success. The nonprofit also sponsors a food & clothing pantry for the emergency needs of women unable to feed their children on the weekends or those who are displaced and hungry.

I have always known that GOD gave me the ability to connect people to others who can provide support. I can remember that early morning that I woke to hear GOD say clearly, YOU ARE A CONDUIT! At first, I was confused, not knowing what this meant, but as I pushed through on my nonprofit journey, I realized that a conduit is a tube that provides protection. It usually has one end that connects to another. **It is a connector!** That's exactly what SLS does. We connect women who are in some of the harshest circumstances to the services that they need.

I also realized that there is POWER in numbers! I reached out to bring women and youth groups, organizations, and nonprofits together to produce collaborative events to empower our communities in a larger way. This allowed me to support both the women and their children. From those outreach efforts, over 25 groups joined *Sisters Lifting Sisters* in forming the Collaborative Initiative. From these collaborations, SLS launched our first Holiday Community Leader Awards Gala. Each nonprofit was able to nominate and recognize individual leaders at this well-attended event. Following our holiday event, we launched *GIRLS to WOMEN* weekend retreats, another collaborative effort. During this event, the collaborative pooled resources to bring empowering education and workshops to each specific group, from *Business Leadership* and *Relationship-Building* workshops to *Etiquette, Avoiding Bullying* and *Mastering College*, the GIRLS to WOMEN events drew hundreds. While *Sisters Lifting Sisters* was the catalyst, collaboration was the key. These events bring youth and women's groups from numerous states together for a day of empowerment workshops to build women and girls holistically.

One of our largest events is our yearly sponsorship of UNC Horizon's in-house rehabilitation residents and their children. These women are provided apartment residence, to assist them to escape domestic violence and rehabilitate from drug abuse. Many have children, but no resources. For six years, *Sisters Lifting Sisters* sponsored their Christmas celebration, providing a catered luncheon for all 50+ women and their children; providing gifts for everyone and even providing Santa Claus to hear the requests of children and for picture taking. Every event is so special and usually brings the volunteers to tears. SLS seeks to create a sense of normalcy and an opportunity for the mothers and their children to create a "good" holiday memory.

Currently, SHERO Publishing is a key sponsor for SLS, as we continue to support monthly lunches for the homeless. To date, SLS has reached women across numerous countries and given back to support over 5,000 single mothers and youth, winning awards for community outreach and service. If I can empower women and let them know that they not alone and help them to see the SHERO with, then my service is not in vain!

Tips for Nonprofit Success:

- **Create a Collaborative Coalition-** I firmly believe that nothing GREAT is birthed alone. When I launched **Sisters Lifting Sisters,** my desire was to find a way to bring synergy to the amazing gifts and talents of community leaders throughout the North Carolina. I started reaching out to youth and women groups to share my vision and our 25-group *Collaborative Coalition* was birthed. While we all had varying initiatives and community outreach efforts, our joint efforts allowed us to impact the community and state in a much greater way. Collaboration is key. Don't be afraid to pool resources and efforts for success.

- **A Solid Team is Essential-** Your board and volunteers are essential to the strength and success of your nonprofit and overall community impact. Pray for God to send you the right people, with the right heart. Seek out people who are willing and ready to serve. When you align your vision with the right community leaders, your nonprofit will thrive.

- **Your Nonprofit Will Evolve-** Your initial vision for your nonprofit will guide the creation and initial outreach efforts, but over time, your mission and even those who support you will change and shift, expect this. As your nonprofit services and outreach evolve, so will your volunteers and sponsors. Sometimes that evolution is essential for long-term success.

- **Never Forget WHY you Started**- I would do you a disservice if I said that nonprofit work was all positive days filled with the joy of serving and giving, with no headaches. On the hard days, always remember, anything GREAT that you do, will always have peaks and valleys.

- **Seek Out Sponsorships-** When you are new to the nonprofit world, you are often hesitant to seek out financial support. Often, you launch your nonprofit, pouring your personal funds into supporting your mission and giving to others. Try to avoid doing this for an extended period of time. It is essential to network, apply for community grants, ask for donations and gain sponsorships. When you are fearless in sharing your vision, the funds will start flow.

No matter what you face, always know what you have the ability to impact others!

Personal Reflections/Notes
Nonprofit Wisdom & Insights

Author Jaemellah Kemp

Author Jaemellah Kemp

Jaemellah Kemp is a Georgia native schooled in the greater Washington, D.C. area and she has a passion for is all things nonprofit management.

Ms. Kemp holds an Associate's degree in Business Administration and a Bachelors in Business Management from the University of Phoenix. She obtained her masters in Nonprofit & Association Management from the University of Maryland University College (UMUC) on May, 2014.

Ms. Kemp joined the UMUC alumni association and recorded a UMUC *My Moments* YouTube video and commercial that aired regionally. She participated in this ad campaign for three years with marketing banners displayed Baltimore Washington International Thurgood Marshall Airport, on the sides of Metro buses, and featured in D.C. area train stations. Ms. Kemp received the 2015 Achiever's Award at UMUC's 25th Annual Alumni Awards in June 2015. In June 2015, she was appointed to UMUC's Board of Directors as the Vice President of the Programming Committee. Ms. Kemp was spotlighted in 2018 as a University System of Maryland (USM) entrepreneur at the USM Chancellor's home for her leadership through **IT TAKES TWO, INC** and its impact on local communities.

In 2012, Ms. Kemp's personal struggles as a single parent and desire to help others led to the birth of **IT TAKES TWO, INC**, a 501c3 public charity. The cornerstone of the organization is its Tools for Success Scholarship. To date, 25 scholarships totaling $8300 have been awarded to local youth living in single parent homes in select Maryland counties.

She decided to combine "doing good" and her education to assist other nonprofit founders through her nonprofit start up consulting firm, *Jaemellah Kemp Consulting, LLC*, that launched in May 2014. Ms. Kemp uses her classroom teaching and daily experiences as a nonprofit leader to help community-minded entrepreneurs to launch sustainable nonprofit organizations.

It's a Birthing Process

The birth of *IT TAKES TWO, INC* was personal. In 2004 I was a twenty-three years old, single parent, raising a black boy and making a little over minimum wage. I was not exactly ready for the responsibility of motherhood, but I embraced it because I was now responsible for another human being. Through my excitement of being a new mom, I started to understand the assignment I had been given while having self-sabotaging thoughts about being a single parent and yet another "statistic". This was by no means the future I had imagined, but God does all things well. It took a few years to realize the blessings my son possessed, but when the manifestation started, I began to birth new things.

Money was always tight even before I had my son, so it was even more stressful afterward. At the time, I could not afford food for the week and school supplies to send him to kindergarten. I received help from family and some friends, but in the midst of the storm, God gave me the vision to help other single parents who also were struggling to make ends meet. While I knew what God was calling me to do, I didn't move as instructed until two years later. I didn't deem myself qualified nor think that I had ample time to run a business while working and going to school full time, making sure my son made it to football and track practice on time, with very little gas some days, and just trying to figure out this mom thing. As we often do, I talked myself out of my own blessing, but finally, in 2012, I took the leap of faith and launched *IT TAKES TWO, INC.*

As I think back, the first year in service was filled with some amazing highs like awarding four inaugural *Tools for Success Scholarships.* The scholarship was awarded to students in grades four through college living in single parent homes to cover back-to-school costs. The funding was provided by one of our founding board members and I remember the conversation clearly even to this day. He used money from his savings to sow a seed into good ground and simply because he believed in the vision. This was a tremendous blessing and the birth of the cornerstone of our organization. The scholarship program has been running for eight years, and to date, we have awarded 25 scholarships totaling $8300.

I can recall our first event, *Fear is No Fun*, an anti-bullying seminar, being a sold-out event after interviewing on WHUR to promote it. Our board members even acted out a skit to enhance the experience, students in attendance were engaged and attentive and the parents and community leaders provided great feedback. It was indeed a memorable yet educational event. Then came the gut-wrenching, almost throw-in-the-towel lows. Before launching the organization, I created a list of ten people that I knew would support in some capacity: donations, words of encouragement, offer to volunteer, something. No one showed up. I'll admit, this just about took me out. I did not come to terms with it until just a couple of years ago when I heard God say, "I didn't give them the vision." Whoa, right? Now, I no longer fault those that do not support the vision simply because they may not be on the same assignment or they are only meant to stay for a little while. In this journey, however, God has brought us every single person needed to grow the vision and they have been complete strangers. This was the first of many lessons learned out of this birthing process - **your help will not look like what you expect**; therefore, be mindful of your interactions with people and use discernment for your blessing could be the very next person you meet.

While this is my journey of impact, we all have a story, so your journey will be different from mine; however, there are things that we will have in common as we birth visions and watch them grow. If you talk with any nonprofit founder, you will find a common theme of - *I wish I had known this before I started* or we have learned to *fail forward* as so eloquently coined by John Maxwell. At some point, we have made some mistakes, poor judgment calls, and realized some truths within ourselves that have made our organizations healthier and foundationally sound. Here are some things this journey has taught me.

1. **Be Very Clear on W.H.Y.**- Who you want to serve (who is your passion population)? How do you plan to serve them? Why you are starting the nonprofit? I was super clear on who we wanted to serve because I was the passion population; a single parent trying to simply make it. Initially, all I sought to do was to award scholarships that paid for school supplies, books, and uniforms. We later added sports and academic registration fees as these are luxuries for families that struggle to put food on the table. Our lawyer offered other objectives as she drafted our Articles of Incorporation and Bylaws (at no cost) to meet students' needs in a more comprehensive manner, so we incorporated a youth program and initiative that awards school supplies for the entire school year. Lastly, my reason for starting IT TAKES TWO, INC is simple: we want to see our young people win despite the economic

and social challenges they face. Being able to articulate your *why* is important to donor communications, public support of the vision, and rallying a team of supporters to grow the organization.

2. **Healthy Nonprofits Have Healthy Boards**- The Board of Directors is the required governing body of a nonprofit organization, but it is also the heartbeat in which the mission needs to thrive. Finding a qualified team can be challenging, but it is possible.

Like myself, most founders tend to look to their trust circle – friends and family. Our founding board was comprised of two church members and a co-worker. But, as I tell my clients, everyone connected to the vision must bring something to the table and that was no different for us. One was n Human Resources professional, the other was a District of Columbia Public Schools teacher and a graphic designer. Perfect combination of talent for a new organization! However, this is not always the right path to success, and I encourage founders to see beyond their immediate circle and look in more professional networks such as LinkedIn and those who serve in your industry. The board should be representative of the community, population served, and possess skill sets and talents needed to launch and grow the vision. Skillsets should be complementary to your own to prevent duplication of skills and provide an opportunity for everyone to operate in their lane. These individuals should have a heart to serve and align with the mission most importantly. This work that we do is passion work and it needs a body of people dedicated to its success while improving the lives of those the organization seeks to serve.

3. **Doing Good is a Business**- You're a do-gooder, like me, and simply want to do good. Our goal is to serve and see the ROI – *Return on Impact* – however, it is important to know that a nonprofit organization is a business and we must operate as such. This means structure, compliance, fiscal responsibility, governance, planning, strategy, intentionality, and execution. Accountability and transparency are synonymous with nonprofits. The state and federal government are holding us accountable as well as our service population, donors, partners, and community at large. Remember, we have voluntarily raised our hands to serve; therefore, we must do our due diligence to be educated and informed about the sector, what is expected of us as leaders, and what we can expect from the industry. This may equate to hiring a consultant, seeking pro bono support from local universities or business incubators, conducting research, speaking with other nonprofit founders, and volunteering with an established organization. For us, I learned the business aspect by obtaining a Masters in Nonprofit and Association

Management. I'm able to use what I learned in the classroom and working for a nonprofit over the past ten years to lead *IT TAKES TWO, INC.* Finally, as with any business, there are associated costs; consequently, we cannot do everything for free, nor can we expect everything for free. Without this understanding, doing good on a shaky foundation diminishes the impact.

4. **There's No Perfect Timing**- I don't believe there is a perfect time, but I believe there is a right time to launch your vision. Remember, I sat on the vision for two years. That simply meant that 2010 wasn't the time, but in the same sense that 2004 was God's appointed time for me to birth my son, 2012 was another birthing year. The vision kept coming back in different forms – dreams of awarding scholarships, feeling that spiritual nudge to move, the scholarship structure started to become clearer, and receiving free filing help from our lawyer. That really was the defining moment that *now* is the time. In making your decision, assess the current state of your life and ask some hard-hitting, "gut check" questions:

Am I really ready to commit to a life of service?
Do I have the time, resources or energy?
Have I considered potential team/board members?
Am I passionate about the work I am about to initiate?
Am I mentally and emotionally available?
Am I motivated and ready to fail and continue to press on?
Am I willing and ready to actually serve and succeed?

If you can honestly answer "yes" to all or most of these questions, and God has told you it's time, then it's time! Trust the process and know that for every vision, He will provide the provision. He just needs your *yes*.

5. **"You Cannot Give from Empty"** - I don't know who coined this phrase, but it is 1000% true. Know your limits. There will be times when you feel lonely, depleted, and utterly frustrated. If I sold you a story of *everything will always be great* and *you'll never experience valley moments*, I would be doing you a major disservice. Operating and leading a nonprofit can be taxing. I remember a few years ago I fell into a bout of depression for about two months. I was hesitant to call it what it was because there was no way that as strong as I was supposed to be that I had to take off the cape, bear my soul, and admit that I was depleted. I had nothing else to give. I took the necessary time to recalibrate, replenish, and renew my commitment. I must say that passion was the driving force. Passion got me up and out of the bed because our youth needed school supplies, books, uniforms, educational

programming, words of encouragement, and parents needed financial relief. In other words, they needed the organization that said they would help, to show up and do just that. These moments are preventable by creating and maintaining a schedule, delegating tasks, engaging in self-care activities, and being honest with yourself and your team.

       6. **You Have the Opportunity to Bless Someone Daily-** For every valley experience, there are mountaintop victories tenfold. The impact you create will have an everlasting effect on those whom you serve. Creativity is limitless in how you accomplish this as long as it is mission- minded. As founders, leaders, and executives, we want to see the mission at work, changing lives, improving neighborhoods, and promoting positive change. Communities depend on nonprofits to do important work, so when we can create joy, opportunities, growth, and success, that in itself is a blessing and a part of the birthing process. This work has many rewards and we must share these stories often for inspiration. We are blessed to have many stories of impact. Mikeya Dunnigan is one such story. She is a two-time *Tools for Success Scholarship* recipient and she has become family. In addition to scholarship awards, we've been invited to her high school graduation, family birthday celebrations, and stay up to date on her academic journey, which culminates next spring as she graduates from Michigan State University with her Masters in Psychology.

       There are many more lessons learned and stories of impact to come as we continue our work. As you birth and nurture your nonprofit vision, your journey will include its own successes and opportunities for growth. Be encouraged with the assignment and know that it requires determination, commitment, drive, and a pure heart. In the same way that God knew I was the right person to birth IT TAKES TWO, INC, He's just as intentional in knowing that you are specifically chosen to impact the world because now it's your time to enter the birthing process.

Personal Reflections/Notes
Nonprofit Wisdom & Insights

Author Kaprece James

Author Kaprece James

Kaprece is a native of Conway, South Carolina. She attended Conway public schools graduating from Conway High School in 2001. Kaprece began collegiate studies at Johnson and Wales University. She completed her studies at Savannah State University, graduating Magna Cum Laude with a Bachelor of Science in Political Science. She has a master's degree from Keller Graduate School of Management in Public Administration and has completed her doctoral education from Walden University. Upon completion of her dissertation, Kaprece will have a Doctorate in Public Policy and Administration with a specialization in nonprofit board governance and fund development.

Kaprece has spent a lifetime of service to her community, both local and military. Service to the local community included work with the NAACP, where she served as president of the college chapter at Savannah State and as president of the Youth and College Division for the state of Georgia. She has also provided service to the local community while clerking for a superior court judge in Savannah, GA. She has provided mentorship to the Frederick, MD community in the form of youth development, social advocacy, and physical and mental health. Kaprece has also advocated for literacy programs of youth and focused on homelessness in Monterey, CA. Currently, Kaprece serves her local community as a Commissioner for Charles County where she is on the Commission for Women. In that capacity she advocates and educates for the rights of women and youth.

Service to the military community has taken many forms as well. She has served as a L.I.N.K.S. Mentor and trainer for spouses and families and First Vice President of Officer Spouses Club while in Twentynine Palms, CA. Kaprece has served as Family Readiness Advisor for recruiting families while in Frederick, MD and as a Family Readiness Officer and Community Liaison and Auction Chair for Marine Officer Spouses' Club while in Okinawa, Japan. She currently serves as the Corresponding Secretary for the Marine Officer Spouses Club of the District of Columbia.

Kaprece is a member of a number of national, civic, and fraternal organizations. She first became a collegiate member of Delta Sigma Theta Sorority Incorporated where she served as president. She currently is a member of the Tri-County Maryland Alumnae Chapter and serves as the Second Vice President. She is a member of Order of Eastern Star where she has served as the Community Liaison. She is a member National Naval Officers Association where she has helped to develop professional training for spouses of service members and served as a mentor for service members. She is a member of the Daughters of Imperial Court, where she has served as president of the local chapter in Okinawa, Japan and served the local Okinawan and military community with local and military family resources. She is a member of Southern Maryland Chain (MD) Chapter of The Links Incorporated, where she serves as the International Trends and Services Chair and Technology Co-Chair. Kaprece is also the Membership Chair for the Savannah State University National Alumni Association Chapter of District of Columbia.

Kaprece is the recipient of a number of awards and recognitions to include: the President's Lifetime Service Award, given by President George W. Bush, the Citizen of the Year Award, the United Way Hall of Champions award, and the Armed Forces Insurance Military Spouse of the Year 2019 for Naval Postgraduate School Monterey. She loves traveling, scuba diving, and mentoring youth.

She is married to Rodney James, an active duty Marine Officer. They currently reside in Charles County, MD.

Following God's Plan

N ot everyone starts a nonprofit for the same reason. Some are responding to a crisis or traumatic event, some a cause or issue, and some believe they have been placed on a path following God's will. At no point during my early years did I think I would be sitting here in 2020 with a four-year-old, 501c3 nonprofit organization, **Stella's Girls, Incorporated,** operating across three continents and seven countries, having served over one thousand girls and women with an all-volunteer staff. After working so hard to follow the professional footsteps of my late grandfather, Cleveland Stevens, ESQ and my role model, Attorney Johnnie Cochran, by getting into law school and becoming a *Civil Rights Attorney and the 1st Black Female Supreme Court Justice,* how did I end up here? It all began with my late great-grandmother Estelle 'Stella' B. Weaver (Granny) (1925-2011).

Molding Me to Lead

Granny was a wife, mother of five, grandmother of fifteen, great-grandmother of fifteen, and great-great-grandmother of two, with an eighth-grade education. It was she who introduced me to service at the age of seven years old through visiting the Conway Nursing Center, in Conway South Carolina, on Saturday mornings. As the only seven-year-old girl in the center, I felt empowered to push residents from their room to the hall for devotion with Granny. Many would have conversations with me, and I learned that most did not receive many visitors, much less visits from grandchildren. I became known as everyone's grandchild as I read, played checkers, and became a master at BINGO with the residents.

At age nine, my involvement with the Center increased. As President of the Youth Council at church, I organized Christmas Caroling by our Children's Choir, toiletry drives, and Adopt-a-Senior Days. This continued until the death of my great-uncle who passed at the Center when I was thirteen. Finding it too painful to return to the Center, Granny and I began to focus on homelessness and eventually advocating against racism in the community. Together, we fed, clothed, and prayed with individuals dealing with abuse, drugs, and homelessness. Granny was a light of hope. Individuals would pop up to her house, even in the middle of the night, and she would always open the door and minister to them. As for me, Granny always reminded me - *To Pray, Study the Word, Get My Education, and Serve Others.*

Calling All Colors

During the spring of 1992, I experienced my first bout with racism with my third-grade teacher. Before entering her class, I was a straight A honor roll student and after the fall semester she had me questioning my ability to learn and make good grades as she had given me mostly C's. My third grade was not shaping up as I thought it would and it changed my outlook as a little black girl in Conway. After talking with several of my classmates and to our parents, we decided that the teacher was the issue and needed to be removed from the school. Racial tension in the school heightened and, though I vaguely remember the full discussion, our Principal and School Board called a mandatory meeting in the school cafeteria to discuss differences and why it was important to respect others. Teachers were also to be held to this standard. A spring conference for teachers took place at our local university, Coastal Carolina, to focus on the role of educators in healing racism.

Recognizing the racial tension, one of my white classmates approached the organizer of the teachers' conference to host one for youth. Together, my classmate and I organized our first, "Calling All Colors Summit" to address racial issues within our school. During this conference, we developed plans and calls to action for our community to come together to fight our racist southern past and to embrace our differences and cultures. It was this moment that turned me into an early civil rights activist and on a path to become a Civil Rights Attorney. This conference still exists today, as we are still battling the same issues.

Savannah State University → Military Spouse → Founder & CEO

Fast forward to 2002 with me attending Savannah State University, working towards my political science degree and my goal of becoming a civil rights attorney and the first black female Supreme Court Justice. I planned every step of my time from serving as President of the Georgia Youth & College Division for NAACP to working as a law intern at the Chatham County Superior Court. I spent time volunteering in my black community, *educating* others on their civil rights and liberties, providing voter education, and hosting mayoral debates. I studied continuously for the LSAT to ensure that I got into my grandfather's alma mater, Howard University School of Law. I graduated from Savannah State, Magna Cum Laude in December 2005, with my eyes set on law school in the fall of 2006. So, what happened?

A United States Marine decided to change his major to political science. Sergeant James popped up in my class in 2004, we began dating in 2005, and we got married in 2006. I became an active duty military spouse. In April 2007 I had already applied and was accepted, to law school. We also moved to our first duty station together in California. While focusing on starting school in the fall of 2007, we learned that he would be deploying to Iraq in February of 2008. After multiple conversations, praying, crying, and frustration, I decided to sacrifice my dream for law school and go with "Plan B". I decided to focus on my passion for serving the community and getting my Master's in Public Administration with a concentration in Nonprofit Leadership. My master's thesis project was to start a 501c3, which put the thought in my head in 2008.

Learning the operations

Graduating Magna Cum Laude in December 2008, I immediately started on my Ph.D. in Public Policy and Administration with my dissertation focused on nonprofit board governance and fund development. Concurrently, I was the Volunteer Station Chair for the American Red Cross on the base, managing over one hundred volunteers, five volunteer programs, and launching my first youth group, *Young Leaders Emerging,* with military teens. Moving to Maryland in 2010, I continued working on my Ph.D., and was now the Director of the Boys & Girls Club in Frederick County working with vulnerable middle school teens. My focus was on *empowering* my teens to become leaders in their school.

Laying the Angel to Rest

On September 16, 2011, I received the call I had been dreading all my life. My granny had finally gained her wings. It was my duty to put her obituary and program together. While writing her eulogy, which I framed after Proverb 31: Virtuous Woman, I started to reflect on how I wanted to be remembered when it was my time to go. After her death, I poured my pain into my community work and was involved in politics, domestic violence programs, feeding the community campaigns, health awareness campaigns, and strengthened my work with vulnerable youth populations. From these different experiences, I learned how nonprofits were structured differently, how boards were governed, how to run successful fundraising campaigns, how to use advocacy to further your mission, and how to recruit and retain volunteers.

In 2012, while working as a Life Skills Trainer at Naval Support Activity Bethesda, I was handed the Family Plus Collaboration, managing over fifty nonprofit organizations. In this role, I held monthly meetings to discuss the services each organization had to offer. We would plan quarterly resource fairs and events for wounded warriors and their families. From this experience, I learned how to network, develop strong partnerships to build a sense of community, and deliver impactful programs. By the end of 2013, I knew my purpose was to be in the community.

Welcome to Liberia

Also in 2012, I attended an event that led me to become a Founding Member of the Board of Directors, and Board Secretary, for B4YT, Incorporated, a 501c3 nonprofit and recognized Liberian nongovernmental organization focused on using arts as a means of advocacy for youth. For the next two years, my role was to strengthen the board and travel back and forth to Liberia to evaluate our program and metrics. During my travels, I noticed that our girls were not being aggressive or truly focused on their opportunities to attend and finish school. I started focusing more on mentorship for the girls and focusing on programs to talk about the stigma, taboos, and lack of opportunities the girls were truly facing in the country. I did this through 2014 when we left Maryland after receiving orders to Okinawa, Japan.

Konnichiwa

By March 2014, we were in Okinawa. Though I already had a job connecting military families with resources, nonprofits, and programs available for them, I also began plugging into the local Okinawan community. This landed me at the AmerAsian School of Okinawa, conducting programs with girls' grades first to eighth. In 2016, I walked away from my government job and decided I would take the year off to focus on finishing my Ph.D. During this time God spoke to me and said, "Who have you dedicated your life to?" and I immediately blurted out, "Granny". The next thought was- I AM A STELLA'S GIRL. With that thought, I focused on writing out my strategic plan and identifying who my board members would be for my founding board. Using the research from my dissertation on the sustainability of nonprofits that have been around for over one hundred years and from my experience working with over thirty different organizations, I knew exactly what I needed to start my nonprofit.

Birthing of Stella's Girls

Fast forward again to 2020. I am the thirty-seven-year-old Founder and President of **Stella's Girls Incorporated,** a nonprofit with a mission to educate and empower young girls and women to become leaders, social change agents, and advocates in their community. I have Chapters in the United States, Liberia, and Japan, and programs in Uganda, Sierra Leone, Nigeria, Ivory Coast, and a pilot program in Rwanda. I have a remarkably diverse team of women, men, and girls. Today, I can say I feel truly blessed for the path and work we are doing as a small nonprofit with a current yearly budget of less than thirty thousand dollars and an all-volunteer staff.

Seven Tips for Nonprofit Beginners

1. **Understand Your Purpose** – Before you begin your nonprofit you first need to know if you are starting your nonprofit for the right reasons and not reacting to a moment or because you think you can compete with a similar nonprofit. This job is not a luxury one and only the servant leaders will survive beyond the normal five-year death sentence of a nonprofit.

2. **Walking Your Path** – Your journey will not be mine, but I am reminded of Jeremiah 29:11 *For I know the plans I have for you, declares the LORD, plans for welfare and not for evil, to give you a future and a hope.* When God is determined for you to walk down the right path, no matter how much you try to stay on your own path, God will send signs that you may ignore until you can no longer ignore them and walk down the path that was set just for you.

3. **Don't Be Afraid to Use Your Skills and Expertise for You** – After 25 years of volunteering and working for other nonprofits, I realized that I had an invaluable skill set that no other organization could afford. I served in every nonprofit position from volunteer to staff to board member to now founder and president. Leveraging what I learned has given me the confidence to grow my nonprofit at the right pace and remind myself that when I don't have the support from my family and friends, I will be able to survive because I have trained myself for the good and bad times of running a nonprofit.

4. **Utilize Every Opportunity and Collaborate for Growth** – Taking advantage of opportunities that have come my way from attending nonprofit conferences, start-up events in San Francisco, long flights to Liberia, a Pan-African Retreat to Uganda, and plugging with the who's who in the community has allowed me to learn, master networking skills, and grow my nonprofit in four years. As a military spouse, having to rebuild my local network every two to four years due to military moves, this has been useful. I leveraged these opportunities to land my first large grant in the amount of thirty thousand dollars to run a summer camp for youth at California State University Monterey Bay in 2019.

5.   **Education and Research Are Key** – No you don't need a Master's or Ph.D. in public administration, but it is helpful to take plenty of courses on operating and financing a nonprofit, plus learning about the federal and state laws to maintain tax-exempt status.

6.   **Building the Right Board** – After years of being in the nonprofit field, board members are always the toughest discussion. As the founder, it is your responsibility to educate your board on the mission, vision, and objectives of your nonprofit. Ensuring your board has governing documents and can work as an effective leadership team is critical to your success. Your board should be focused on developing a wider and broader perspective, from monitoring the organization's efforts to strategically planning the organization's response to the future. When picking your board identify people you trust and have skills in finance, project management, tax law, marketing, and a subject matter expert aligned with the organization's mission.

7.   **Volunteers are the Bloodline** – Having a reliable team of volunteers is the crucial key to a nonprofit's success. There is never a shortage of volunteers, but most of them are untapped, waiting to serve, and waiting for someone to ask them. Before you begin recruiting your volunteers ensure you identify your needs, select a volunteer coordinator, involve your board and staff, and have screening, legal, and safety policies. Once you land your volunteers learn why they want to volunteer, their goals, and assign a role beneficial to them. Most volunteers will tell you they do not do it for recognition, but please recognize and reward your volunteers for their invaluable work. If you have staff be sure they have a working relationship with the volunteers.

Stay Focused

Being a founder of a nonprofit is lonely until you find your crew. If you pour your heart, soul, and dedication into your nonprofit you will see the benefits and impact of the community you serve. Remember to always learn, find a mentor, share successes and failures, have fun, and collaborate with others to continue moving your mission forward.

Personal Reflections/Notes
Nonprofit Wisdom & Insights

_____

_____

_____

_____

_____

_____

_____

_____

_____

_____

_____

Personal Reflections/Notes
Nonprofit Wisdom & Insights

Author Keva Brooks Napper

Author Keva Brooks Napper

An icon of strength and resiliency, Keva Brooks Napper is a powerhouse entrepreneur based in North Carolina. Keva is a two-time Best Selling Author, Speaker, and Humanitarian. She is the Founder of MEEK Legacy, LLC, a family inspired company that supports her mission of inspiring and uplifting through film, literature, and speaking. Her most recent projects include "Invisible Hope" and "Truth of Thorns," for which she holds creator, writer, and producer credits.

For a total of 17 years, Keva has been thriving through Lupus and desires to see others battling any type of invisible illness do the same. To this end, she founded *Beautiful Butterflies Inc.*, a nonprofit foundation used to bring awareness and education on Lupus and other illnesses. She often says, "I can't eradicate illness but I can help eradicate the pain of it," and shapes her endeavors with this in mind.

Keva's academic repertoire includes a Bachelor of Arts degree in Elementary Education with a minor in English from North Carolina Central University. Throughout the years, she has received a myriad of awards for her service and brilliance as a community leader. Some of those honors include: Teacher of the Year, Guilford County's Reader's Choice Best Writer, Women in Organizing -- Sheroe Award, and ACHI Non-profit Executive Director of the Year Award.

Beautiful Butterflies Inc. is a 501c3 non-profit lupus foundation founded by Keva Brooks Napper in 2011. Our sole purpose is to provide support, services, and education to those affected by lupus, primarily minorities. *Beautiful Butterflies Inc.* pursues this mission through: supporting individuals with lupus, their families, friends, and caregivers; and advocating for increased public and private sector support for research on lupus; heightening awareness of the impact and effects of lupus.

Learn more about Keva at www.mybeautifulbutterflies.com
Twitter: @keva_diva/ Facebook – @keva.napper
Instagram- @keva_diva1 / @mybeautifulbutterflies / @my_bbi

Do You See What I See?

It was a Sunday Morning and church was packed. I sat on the second row behind my parents, the Bishop and First Lady, and our guest preacher. My mom kept looking back at me asking, "Are you okay?". She sensed something was wrong, but each time I would shake my head in the affirmative, "Yes I'm fine." The choir sang, but today I didn't get up and clap. I sat and barely moved. Our sanctuary seats 3,000 people; yet as I looked around, I could only recognize a few people. Even then, I still didn't think anything was wrong. The guest preacher got up to speak and in the middle of his sermon babies from both sides of the sanctuary started to cry. I remember him saying, "Get up and walk the babies," and people kind of laughed, and then my world changed. I started having a grand mal seizure, the strongest type of seizure anyone could have. I had never had a seizure before, so I didn't know what was going on. I started sliding down in the seat, with my arms extended up in the air; I had no control over what my body was doing. My cousin was beside me and tried to grab me. My mom and brother jumped up to assist; while the preacher was still standing, trying to preach to a sanctuary full of people. It was a hectic and scary scene; yet, there was a sense of calmness and order. I was now unconscious. A doctor at the church began to assist until the EMS arrived. I regained consciousness and was confused, frantic, and scared; I was lost. I was taken to the emergency room, only to have more grand mal seizures. The seizures became debilitating; causing me to have an out-of-body experience. I was taken to ICU and placed in a medically induced coma so the doctors could determine the source of the seizures. When I awoke from the coma more than 24 hours later, the neurologist and hematologist explained to me there were two blood clots on the left side of my brain that were the source of the seizures. Ultimately, those clots caused the stroke. I was only 27 years old. My blood pressure wasn't high, cholesterol wasn't high, and none of the classical signs were there. How did this happen?

In 2003, one year before this earth-shattering experience, I was diagnosed with Systemic Lupus Erythematosus (SLE – LUPUS). I chose not to talk about the diagnosis. I took my medicine and went about life as if the diagnosis never existed. I was silent, almost ashamed, to have an incurable disease, that I didn't know much about and didn't know many people with it. What an irony! I privately hid the disease, but guess where it was exposed? You guessed it. Lupus burst forth that Sunday where everybody in church saw me having seizures, and being wheeled out in the middle of the sermon. Grand mal seizures, disease exposure in public, medically induced coma, in the hospital for two weeks, a stroke, and yet, I was able to walk out needing no rehabilitation and having no visible signs of the trauma I had experienced. God is faithful!

After healing from the stroke, I crept into my protective shell. I didn't talk about having Lupus nor did I mention the additional invisible illness diagnosis that was given at the hospital: Protein S Deficiency. That simply means eating too many greens will thicken my blood and cause me to have blood clots. I now have two invisible illnesses, and I'm not really discussing either. I chose to take my meds and keep going on with life as if nothing happened, even though I faced death and 6 months after being released from the hospital, I lost a baby. I had a mouth and working vocal cords but was voiceless.

Fast forward to 2010. I was reading a magazine on lupus and I saw where Toni Braxton was speaking at a luncheon in New York; sharing her story on lupus to an audience of 200 people. I said to myself, I can do that! I can share my truth right here at church; I can educate and bring awareness to my community about my diagnosis. I made the decision that December to host a Lupus Awareness Luncheon in February. We announced it and sold over 200 tickets in two weeks. I was blown away! I realized at that point, this was bigger than me simply sharing my story of my diagnosis. I connected with Mrs. Nancy McLean, a member of the church who had her own non-profit but was known for writing grants and helping others start and apply for non-profits. Nancy was a wealth of knowledge for me. We met and she asked me all the difficult questions. She made sure I understood that this assignment couldn't be about how I felt in the moment because that feeling wouldn't be there every day. There would be tough days, rewarding days, sad days, happy days, confusing days, and days when I would see that it was worth it all. She made me understand that this is a calling and an assignment, not just something established to give you a prestigious title. Nancy pushed me and challenged me and made me dig deep, and once I had an understanding, we applied for the 501c3. At that time, most people were getting their papers back in six months to a year. We received ours in less than six weeks. **Beautiful Butterflies, Inc.** was born!

Our first luncheon was exactly what it was purposed to be. It was educational; providing awareness and exposure of Lupus to the community. Many attendees didn't know what Lupus was, who it affects, and how to support those who have been diagnosed. We were able to share stories, have a doctor present information and allow companies to provide resources. I was able to finally release my voice. This was the first time I publicly shared my diagnosis. I was no longer voiceless, instead I was now an advocate with an entire community supporting me. Going through a metamorphosis like that of the caterpillar; I was shedding my cocoon.

After the great luncheon, the work was just beginning. There were no Lupus support groups within our geographical area. We started a local monthly support group for Lupus Thrivers, family members, friends, co-workers, and caregivers. During our support group meetings, we discovered that there were other invisible illness Thrivers without support groups and we invited them to share in our victory journey. We are on this journey together. Oftentimes, people ask why we say Thrivers and not survivors. We focus on thriving because "To Survive is to Live, but to Thrive is to Excel!" – George W. Brooks. We don't want to just live in life, we want to live and excel in everything we do. We don't want a mediocre life, therefore we do survive, but more importantly we- Thrive!

Along with our support group, we were the first independent Lupus non-profit in the Triad area to have a 5k Lupus Walk, where hundreds would come and Lace up for Lupus! We also held a golf tournament, Family Day at Carowinds, Game Night with the Charlotte Hornets, partnered locally to participate in health fairs, partnered with several HBCUs to educate on the impact of Lupus, gave over 100k in food donations, and partnered with local churches to inform the minority community of the impacts of invisible illnesses. In addition, we held mental health panels to educate on the invisible illness such as Depression and

Anxiety and built strong sustainable relationships with companies who still support our nonprofit.

Doing something new in the community to bring awareness also brought attention and caused some larger organizations to not like what we were doing. Despite the fact that I was becoming a "**Beautiful Butterfly**," there were those who wanted me to stay in a caterpillar position. They didn't like the fact that our organization had started to make an impact in the minority community. These groups didn't want us to educate and bring awareness to how Lupus is two to three more times prevalent among women of color; African Americans, Hispanic/Latinos, Asians, Native Americans, Native Hawaiians. How 9 out of 10 adults with Lupus are women between the ages of 15-44. How 1.5 million people in the United States have been diagnosed with Lupus. How 40% of adults and as many as 66% of all children with Lupus will develop kidney complications. How there is only one FDA approved drug specifically for Lupus. How Lupus is not contagious; It is not Cancer. How it is not like AIDS- the immune system is overactive with Lupus; it is underactive with AIDS. How you can still live a productive life after the diagnosis. We shared the signs and symptoms and how supporters could help those diagnosed. We gave HOPE.

Even with all of the education and hope we were giving, we were still met with opposition. As the leader, I was asked to continue to plan and execute events, bring awareness in the community, but to channel the proceeds to the larger organizations. They wanted to partner with us by letting our foundation do the work, continue to be the hands and feet in the community, but they wanted the reward. They didn't want any of the local Thrivers to receive the assistance. They didn't want our foundation to receive any acknowledgment for community work. We were to put in the blood, sweat and tears, but they wanted to receive all the credit. They wanted to ignore the truth of what the real faces of invisible illnesses looked like. When I refused to become a slave to their system, I was advised they would be watching everything I did. That didn't intimidate me or curtail the work we were doing. It propelled us to continue and go to greater heights. I had to deal with all of this while only a handful of people knew what was going on. I had to continue to smile, continue to serve, continue to plan, continue to create, continue to comfort, continue to educate, continue to inspire, all while refusing to be torn down, intimidated, or forced to abandon the assignment. To this very day, I have been made aware of them "watching" us. We continue to use it as strength for the journey; to know that we must be doing something right.

This was all a part of the metamorphosis that *Beautiful Butterflies, Inc.* would need to go through in order to grow into a mature nonprofit butterfly. *Beautiful Butterflies, Inc.* was birthed from a place within me and designed to educate, provide resources, support, and inspire those challenged by invisible illnesses; especially minorities. Everything has a purpose, a meaning, including the name. *Beautiful Butterflies Inc.* – A butterfly is a symbol of hope, and oftentimes those with Lupus get a butterfly rash. Keva is my name and in the Irish Origin it means Beautiful. My paternal grandmother is part Irish and I wanted to be connected to the name of the foundation, so I named it *Beautiful Butterflies*. Just as the butterfly doesn't start its life as the beautiful being that it is, neither did our foundation. We went through many stages, tests, and trials to get where we are now; continuing to grow. Just as the butterfly starts out as an egg that is laid on a plant and then develops as a larva, grows and transforms and eventually emerges as what we call a caterpillar. This caterpillar will eat the same leaf it was born onto in order to grow. As it grows, it will transform into the pupa. Once the metamorphosis is complete a butterfly will emerge. While the natural eye cannot see the butterfly forming during the metamorphosis stage, we know that the end result will be a *Beautiful Butterfly*. Oftentimes people will look at me and still see the caterpillar I started as. They don't realize the dark place of the cocoon I had to go through to be able to fly in the sky with wings and a different vision. However, there is something called a Butterfly Effect. The Butterfly Effect can change the whole pattern of the world without great fanfare or recognition but it is effective nonetheless. My goal is to be effective regardless of recognition, opposition, or appreciation by those who do not see as I see.

Personal Reflections/Notes
Nonprofit Wisdom & Insights

_____

_____

_____

_____

_____

_____

_____

_____

_____

_____

_____

_____

_____

Author Kiwan Fitch-Webster

Author Kiwan Fitch-Webster

Kiwan N. Fitch-Webster is an Entrepreneur, Published Author of five books, Playwright, Producer, Motivational Speaker, Mentor, Wife, Mother and so much more.

Kiwan has operated in service to others for over 20 years, serving women and families in the Midlands and beyond. She has served by offering women *EmPOWERment,* support, clinical counseling, food, clothing, and assisting with a host of other needs.

In September 2018, Ms. Fitch-Webster launched the *Journey Towards Purpose Program* as a part of the J2P Global Institute. It is with this platform that personal development courses are offered to women in a live and online format. Currently, J2P Global Institute has certified 35 Purpose Coaches in the United States: North and South Carolina, Illinois, New Jersey, Pennsylvania, Georgia. The *Journey Towards Purpose Program* is also in operation in London, England.

As a way to consolidate her life of service, in June of 2019 Kiwan joined the management team of Hannah House, a Christ Central Ministries transitional housing unit. There she serves as General Manager, while also running her personal and professional development company, *Journey Towards Purpose Global Institute.*

Kiwan is married to Edward R. Webster. She is the mother of three sons, one daughter in love, two bonus sons, two grandsons, and two granddaughters. Hailing from Jersey City, New Jersey, Kiwan made Columbia, South Carolina their home in 2010. She has a Bachelor of Arts degree in Sociology from New Jersey City University. She is currently pursuing a Master's degree in Business Management and Leadership from Webster University.

The Journey Begins

Those little black and white shoes... That's what attracted my mother to private Catholic Schools. She made up her mind before I was born that her children would attend private school. I started Sacred Heart School in September of 1978. And I stayed in private school from kindergarten through the 12th grade when I graduated from the Holy Family Academy in Bayonne, New Jersey in 1990. Holy Family was an all-girls private Catholic School. My graduation was preceded by an experience that shaped the start of my adult life. On May 7, 1990, my father passed away from Acquired Immunodeficiency Syndrome; otherwise known as AIDS. Exactly 25 days before my High School graduation.

I had promised my father I would go to college. It honestly took me many years to realize that his illness and death catapulted me into a black cloud. I truly had no direction. But because of my very disciplined upbringing, I couldn't just continue to wander aimlessly. I had to have a plan to get back on track. So I chose cosmetology. Yes, 12 years of college-prep education and I chose cosmetology. You can understand now why I *had* to promise my father I would still go to college.

Looking back now, I realized that in all of my years, I have never once heard my mom mention that it was a struggle to keep my sister and me in private school. Not one word. Clarence Fitch, on the other hand... "All this money and you want to do HAIR".

After a year and a half in North Carolina, I was a part of Dudley's Cosmetology University's second graduating class. There was no way with all my college prepping that I would attend the *local* cosmetology school in New Jersey. When I look back at that time in my life, I can only shake my head and laugh. I simply squandered much of my inheritance; I spent a lot of money. Lack of direction and a grieving heart were just added pressures that complicated my teen years.

I returned home excited about this new journey of "doing HAIR" but also anxious to get started on Phase Two; fulfilling the promise of going to college. That Fall of 1991, I started college. Before the year was out, I was pregnant with my first child.

Out of necessity, I learned how to hang on and get through college. I dropped classes that were challenging and dropped whole semesters when life was rocky. I just didn't realize that was going to do more than make my degree take longer. I had to reapply and then be a readmit to the university. Hurdle after hurdle; yet I kept going. I did what was asked of me. Now my baby boy was three years old. I was working full time in a hair salon and going to Jersey City State University. Doing what was asked meant I could take 11 credits instead of 12. I was all set up for school and then I went to get my childcare voucher for daycare. Well, I was met with much resistance. I recall asking "What do you mean you can't pay for my childcare; I'm in school" I then asked for a supervisor who proceeded to tell me that because I'm in school part time and not full time- I NO LONGER QUALIFY. WOW, I didn't realize one credit would make that much of a difference in my life. Sitting there refusing to leave without a solution; ANOTHER WORKER, says go to another agency and get a: CWEP PLACEMENT FOR YOUR ADDITIONAL HOURS… (all I could think of is what hours? It's 1 credit short of being in full time status!!) Off I went to begin what was the BEST detour ever. Later that evening, during my client's hair appointment, I discussed my distressing experience at Social Services. This client, I now credit with helping me find my purpose. She referred me to her part time job, at a group home that served boys and girls aged 6 to 12 years old. I began my CWEP experience, COMMUNITY WORK EXPERIENCE PROGRAM at the group home. This CWEP was so much more than work experience. I gained valuable experience, satisfied the welfare qualifications for my child care assistance voucher, and later I was able to use this position for credits at the university. I also used it for my internship for my major. It was so significant that I even changed my major from business to sociology. This detour was a huge pivot that was clearly a GOD setup for my future.

My CWEP placement became a paid position. I went on from there to have several positions in varying nonprofit agencies. I can honestly say that I've worked with EVERYONE. In spring of 2006, my best friend, a few other ladies and I came together to form *My Sistahz Keeper Association (MSKA).* This was a blind attempt to deal with some of the many issues women face. We went from cleaning playgrounds in Newark, New Jersey to supplying battered women's programs with toiletries to getting our 501c3 to formally do those activities and many other needed projects. What was so significant about MSKA was by spring 2006, I had been a single mom for seven years, married, a prison wife, then an abused wife, and then again a single mom with two additional children. I'd come to a place where I wanted my work to have meaning. I loved being the helper. I loved being a walking resource for others. Being a mom of three sons has certainly shaped my purpose. I've been asked why my focus is always women… well HER, I know.

I've asked God if I had to experience everything my clients have experienced in order to have first-hand experience? I even have an experience with Narcotic Anonymous and have never taken any narcotics in my life. You see my father was a Vietnam War veteran. He found a way to deal with the massive destruction and racial tensions of that experience with IV drug use. He became a heroin addict. His use continued once he was back home. The Black GI had a really rough time in the 70s. Drugs, post-traumatic stress and many other demons were hard to deal with. When he finally decided to get clean and live a drug-free lifestyle, Narcotic Anonymous (NA) helped save him. So, as a child I went to NA meetings, I understood the process of working the 12 steps. I understood the confidentiality of it all. I even learned about the locations all around my hometown. All of this information is vital when a client sits before me needing help with addiction. I know you need 90 meetings in 90 days, get a sponsor, and stay away from certain people, places, and things. I've handed out this information countless times. And because it came from such a personal place it was always received with the love it was given.

I've always enjoyed the work. Helping others became my drug of choice. I can recall when that feeling jumped into my spirit. I was around seven years old. A simple desire to play outside with my girlfriend Donna was met with the hurdle of her little brother. You see, Donna's mother was in the hospital and her older siblings had already left home. We had to find clothes for her brother and feed him. Well, this was the first time I had ever done such adult responsibilities unsupervised. Okay, I had never fried bacon on my own. THAT created a feeling inside of me that made me stand up taller. I've chased that feeling of being a helper ever since.

To date, I have personally created a CWEP Community Work Experience Program in New Jersey and also in South Carolina. God has okes. Who would have thought that a CWEP placement in a group home was my very first job in my field of work that would carry me over twenty years?

In 2017 I suffered but survived a massive heart attack. When you experience something of that magnitude it's impossible not to often think of legacy. What am I leaving for my sons and grandchildren? I didn't choose a career path that will make me millions. I did choose a path of purpose and impact. My personal mission statement that I live by is to live a life that impacts lives and have fun doing it. I promised myself that producing THAT legacy is far more meaningful than money.

Personal Reflections/Notes
Nonprofit Wisdom & Insights

_____

_____

_____

_____

_____

_____

_____

_____

_____

_____

_____

_____

Personal Reflections/Notes
Nonprofit Wisdom & Insights

Author Lisa Ambers

Author Lisa Ambers

Lisa Ambers is the Founder and President of *Beyond the Classroom, Inc.*, a 501 (c)(3) nonprofit organization, based in Waldorf, Maryland. She is passionate about exposing children and young adults to people, places, and things they would not normally or easily have access to in their daily lives. Lisa believes that positive exposure is key and provides experiences to empower youth to see the world outside of their classrooms and neighborhoods. *Beyond the Classroom, Inc.* is dedicated in memory of Lisa's father, Thomas "Sonny" Jordan, who instilled in her a strong desire to invest in the youth.

Lisa earned a Bachelor of Science Degree in Human Resource Management from the University of Maryland Global Campus. She is an innovative leader with more than twenty-five years of marketing, event management, and program development experience, having worked at the corporate headquarters for a major hospitality company for over eighteen years. Lisa is currently employed as Vice President of Regional Marketing for a corporate banking institution.

Lisa is a community service advocate who strongly believes in giving back and has served in the following capacities: Deaconess, Women's Ministry Leader, Girls Ministry Leader, and Outreach Ministry member at Tabernacle of Praise, Literacy Chair of Top Ladies of Distinction, Southern Maryland Chapter, Student Mentor at University of Maryland Global Campus, Parent Advisory Council Member, University of Maryland, College Park, PTSO Vice President, and Election Judge.

Living on a Legacy

G rowing up, I did not understand how my spiritual upbringing would impact every aspect of my life. Church was my family's home away from home. We started off with Sunday School, then morning worship service. That was followed by dinner, prepared by the elders of the church. Following dinner, afternoon service could go late into the evening. The delicious home-cooked food was the best part of the day. What I did not realize then is that all those Sundays spent in church would lead me to keep my Daddy's legacy alive today.

My father was the ultimate community servant! I admired how he helped those in need and performed God's work. He always did things to help others: whether that was repairing an appliance, driving neighborhood kids to school events, building props for church plays, singing in the men's choir, or creating a float for a local parade. I remember the feelings of jealousy when he left home to rescue someone else or to do something at the church, but the joy he exuded when he returned home was priceless. It replaced my jealousy with happiness and inspired me at a young age to want to serve others, too. That is when I began to emulate my hero, my Dad.

When I was 12 years old, I joined the Youth Usher Board. Throughout my teen years, I served meals and participated in numerous holiday plays. That passion to serve continued into my adult life where I led the Women's and Girls' Ministries, became a member of the Outreach Committee, and was ordained as a Deaconess. These roles made my Daddy beam with pride and gave me the opportunity to educate others, enhance my leadership skills, and help in ways that not only blessed others, but blessed me in return. Everything in my family centered around the church. However, there were other facets of my life that were instrumental in prompting me to begin this quest to do something greater. People and experiences, good or bad, can help define the path that you take in life.

My Career

My career has also been a major influence on my nonprofit decision. As a child, I wanted to be a school teacher. I could picture myself teaching the students and making my classroom beautiful, especially my bulletin boards. The desire to work with young people existed back then and still exists today. I did not pursue teaching as my career choice because I was encouraged to go to Corporate America for a higher salary and additional advancement opportunities, and that is what I did.

I spent close to 20 years working at the corporate headquarters for a major hotel chain and was exposed to many wonderful experiences. I traveled internationally, stayed at world-class hotels, tried different foods, and experienced premier social functions. I could see the world through my work. Having those experiences gave me the desire to expose youth to the world beyond their communities and give them a global perspective at a younger age. I brought the world to them through unique experiences not knowing this was a trial run for what was about to come.

Being obedient to the voice of God, I shifted directions in my career. I went to work in the banking industry. Now that was a big stretch for me not knowing anything about banking. I attended several seminars on living your purpose at work and I was selected to serve as a strategic advisor for the company's purpose program. I was even recognized for the bank's top award for my job performance and for the work that I did in the community. Look at God...he shifted me to work for a company that reinforced my desire to live my personal purpose and passion. Both of these employment opportunities helped amplify my desire to make a difference in the world. When one door closes, another opens with new opportunities. You have to stay focused and listen to what God tells you to do. He's an on-time God, yes he is.

A Former Pastor

People connected to you can also provide direction on what road you should take. My former pastor preached a series of sermons about living your dreams, starting your own business, or nonprofit and how important it is to give back to others. Those sermons resonated with me and helped me to realize that it was time to stop thinking and waiting and to implement a plan to start my own nonprofit organization. I began to research how to get started. I attended classes at the local library and workshops through nonprofit support organizations, and read a lot of information online. I kept educating myself while I was struggling to keep up with family, work, and church obligations.

My Pastor participated in several events that I held at the church and told me time and time again that I should take my programs to the community to reach more people. One of our most popular events was Vision Board Workshops. I strongly believe in vision boards and how they allow you to put your dreams and aspirations into the atmosphere. Two years before I launched my nonprofit, I put the words "Start a nonprofit organization" on my own vision board. I still have that board and show it to students at current workshops as a testimony of how my vision manifested into reality. I am thankful God used my Pastor to help me realize that there was greater power beyond the four walls of the church; even though the church is a nonprofit and the church family performed community work. My nonprofit would be an additional vessel to help reach even more people.

Life's Distractions

Life can take you on a lot of twists and turns like you are on a roller coaster. You just have to stay strapped in and hold on. And boy did life take me on a ride. The man I admired most, the greatest Daddy in the world, the man who loved life and everybody around him, became ill. It was so painful to see him struggling when he had been such a vibrant and giving person. I had to step up to help take care of him...he became my priority. Trust me, those last two years were some of the best times that I ever spent with my father. We laughed in the car while going to doctor's appointments, had lunch together, looked at the beautiful scenery on the drive and talked about how much he just wanted to go to church and sing in the men's choir.

In addition to my Daddy being sick, other distractions kept coming to throw me off course. I had to become invincible in order to stay focused on my vision and the work that I had to do. My power words became FEARLESS and UNSTOPPABLE. They kept me pushing during this difficult time. My friends and family were there, but I also had to keep encouraging myself.

My Daddy's health kept deteriorating until he was called home to be with the Lord. On the day that he transitioned, I told myself as I was walking out of the hospital, that I had to do something to keep his legacy alive. At the funeral, I was in awe hearing so many people share stories about how he helped them. I had no idea the number of people he touched. I cried as I looked at the words "THE LORD IS IN HIS HOLY TEMPLE" hanging above the choir stand. I remember my Daddy making those letters when I was 13 years old. He wanted them to be perfect back then and they are still perfect today!

Shortly after my Daddy's funeral, I pulled myself together and got my nonprofit in order. *Beyond the Classroom, Inc.* was soon birthed and was dedicated in memory of my father, Thomas Henry Jordan, with the mission to expose children and young adults to people, places, and things that they may have limited or no access to in their daily lives. After many years of preparation, enduring trials and tribulations, my vision came to life. My life was forever changed and now I'M LIVING ON A LEGACY.

I can clearly see now that my Daddy was planting seeds of service in me all those years so that I would grow into the servant leader and community-based teacher that I am today. He was prepping me to be ready to expose thousands of young people to new things through learning workshops, mentoring clubs, educational trips, and community service activities. Watching my vision come to fruition has been so gratifying. I know that Daddy is smiling down from Heaven on how much my nonprofit has progressed over the years. We have certainly grown beyond the four walls of the church with programming in Washington DC, Maryland and Virginia. We will continue to grow in school systems and communities across the country. We will do our part to expose the next generation of youth with the education and experiences to help them live their best lives beyond the classroom.

I am so thankful to every person and experience that inspired me to take this path that I absolutely love! I have the best of both worlds --- I am still active in the church and in the community at the same time! God is so good! Take time to listen and observe what is around you. Do not let life's distractions stop you from walking in your purpose…keep pushing and your vision will become a reality.

Ten Seeds for Success

I am keen about helping others succeed and enjoy sharing my key learnings. It is important to build up others.

- *Be a Visionary:* Take the time to strategize. Get as much education about the nonprofit sector as possible in order to start and sustain your nonprofit. Determine what makes your nonprofit unique and how it can stand out among hundreds of other nonprofits in your community. Create short-term and long-term plans.
- *Recruit and Retain an Engaged Board:* Go through a rigorous process when selecting your Board members. Select those who align with your mission and bring expertise to your nonprofit. Include members with whom you do not have existing personal relationships. They can help bring a neutral perspective to the table. Your Board members have a brand and their reputation can positively or negatively impact your nonprofit. Your Board should also feel comfortable promoting and fundraising for the organization. Set fundraising goals for each member.
- *Refrain from Getting "Founder's Syndrome":* Do not get absorbed in running your organization by yourself. Be sure to delegate to board members and volunteers. Do not sacrifice your mental, physical, or financial well-being.
- *Have a Small Support Circle:* It is vitally important to have a few people in your circle (outside of your Board) who believe in your nonprofit's mission and are there to support you. They can be a listening ear, help vet your ideas and you can call them at any time, even in the middle of the night.
- *Set Goals & Measure Effectiveness:* Determine when to launch new programs and have success metrics in place that will measure the impact your organization is making. This information is needed to secure many grants. Constantly seek out opportunities to learn and grow. This will help eliminate a status quo mentality in your nonprofit. At the end of your fiscal year, document what worked well and areas for improvement.

- *Collaborate with Other Nonprofits:* There are benefits that come from collaborating with other nonprofits which can allow you to reach more participants, help save on program costs, make programming more effective and efficient and allow you to expand your network.

- *Promote Your Nonprofit in All Aspects of Your Life:* You and your Board members are billboards for your nonprofit at work, church, with family, and in the community at large. This is how you can make new connections, recruit volunteers, and collect impromptu donations. Each member should have an elevator speech that explains the "what" and "why" of the organization that is quick and to the point. Personal as well as your nonprofit's social media channels should be utilized for marketing and fundraising.

- *Stay Current in the Nonprofit Space:* Be intentional with on-going learning to stay on top of the ever-changing world. Attend conferences, participate in webinars, sign up with nonprofit support organizations, join groups for nonprofits on social media channels and read blogs. Also stay abreast of current technology and marketing trends. There are plenty of free resources online. Check to see if your local library or community college provides resources and training.

- *Have a Contingency Plan in Place:* This is so important especially with all the changes that took place during the COVID-19 pandemic. You need to be agile and have the ability to pivot quickly when external factors impact your nonprofit.

- *Pay Your Knowledge Forward:* Share your nonprofit knowledge with others and mentor those who are starting out. We are stronger together.

Distractions to Avoid

Distractions will come and can derail you and pull you off course if you allow them. These are some of the distractions that I struggled with most:

- **Work & Family:** Do not allow family and work obligations to stop you from moving forward. Carve out time to work on your nonprofit. That can mean very early in the morning or late at night.
- **Non-Support:** Do not expect everyone to support you and do not let that demotivate you. Look for funding in other ways: secure grants, create a service to collect fees, and be prepared to use your own money when needed.
- **Competition:** There is a lot of competition in the nonprofit world. There are some nonprofits that do not want to collaborate. There are others who act like they support you just to get close enough to see what you are doing then they quickly implement your ideas. Be careful and minimize what critical information you share.

God is doing a great work through me. I encourage those who want to start a nonprofit, to get the ball rolling. For those who already have a nonprofit, keep it going and take it to the next level. Lastly, for those who just want to give back to others, be a blessing. Sow your seeds and you will leave your legacy behind.

Give, and it will be given to you. A good measure, pressed down, shaken together and running over, will be poured into your lap. For with the measure you use, it will be measured to you. Luke 6:38 (NIV)

Personal Reflections/Notes
Nonprofit Wisdom & Insights

_____

_____

_____

_____

_____

_____

_____

_____

_____

_____

_____

_____

Author Lori Pratico

Author Lori Pratico

Lori Pratico began her artistic career when she was nineteen years old as a billboard artist in Philadelphia. She grew up in a row home in the city and remembers dreaming of a day she'd drive down the street and be able to point and say, "I did that." Self-taught and full of ambition, she learned from unique experiences that pushed her outside of her own boundaries and the boundaries of society. Today, Lori's artwork is recognized on a national level. Her work has been represented by galleries and shown at Art Basel, an international art fair. She's painted live at the Hard Rock Hotel and Casino, the world-renowned Miami Boat Show, and the Chicago and Philadelphia Travel and Adventure Shows. Her artwork has been published in Marie Claire, Juxtapoz, and Professional Artist magazines. Lori has been invited to speak at numerous community and art events including Art Fort Lauderdale, and the Women's Studies Program at Old Dominion University. In 2020 she curated an all-women's national gallery show called "Persistence" in Norfolk, Virginia. and was awarded the Artist Visionary Award in Broward County, Florida where she now lives with her greatest creation, twenty-eight-year-old twins Grace and Gianni, as well as her fiancé, Diane.

Lori is a resident artist at Art Serve, Inc. Fort Lauderdale, and serves on Broward County's Public Arts and Design Committee. Lori also leads programming at The Coral Springs Museum of Art where she brings art to children with Autism, Cerebral Palsy and other special abilities, and has served as Art Director for the Florida Youth Pride Coalition serving LGBTQ+ youth.

A philanthropist at heart, Lori's success in art led her to use her talents in 2015 as a vehicle to launch the **Non-Profit Girl Noticed, Inc.** This non-profit is a community based arts outreach program that through self-discovery uncovers and showcases the unique strengths, contributions and abilities of females, providing positive and empowering art experiences that help to define each girl's value in society. She has completed over thirty-five murals in fifteen states celebrating and advocating for girls and women of all ages, and continues to work rigorously on programming to further her cause.

info@girlnoticed.org / www.girlnoticed.org

Girl Noticed

There is a photo taped to my studio wall behind my easel that I look at often. The photo is of a seven-year-old girl. She is sitting proudly on her banana seat bicycle, arms raised in the air, fist clenched. She looks like she could take on the world, or at least any other seven-year-old and their bike. She is a badass. She is me.

Age seven is also about the time I began to lose sight of the little girl who is in that picture. My grip on innocence had begun to slowly slip away, and I could no longer hold onto the wonderment of who I would become or who I was. I was taught and heard repeatedly two things growing up, *I shouldn't*, and *I couldn't*. The circumstances and stories of why I never felt good enough or why being me was unacceptable are long and somewhat tedious to tell, so I'll summarize like many women do, and label it under "things I only tell my therapist."

There was one aspect of being me that I managed to hold onto as a kid and to this day have never let go of. I would be, and in many ways already was, an artist. I was five when my kindergarten teacher slipped a smock over my head, stood me in front of an easel and told me I could put my fingers in the paint. Finger painting was the single most amazing thing in the world. I was encouraged to make a mess on both me and the paper, and I believed both finished products were uniquely beautiful.

I was not the best artist, I was certainly not what most people would have considered naturally talented, but I loved the freedom to create, and I did whenever I could. I wasn't able to draw things right from my head. For example, if you asked me to draw a rabbit, it would probably turn out looking like a cat with long ears, but with practice I became very good at drawing what I saw, copying what was in front of me. By the time I was a teenager I could draw a person exactly as they looked, which seemed to be the subject matter I gravitated to. I became better and better at drawing faces and capturing a person's likeness. Soon I'd begin to also capture a feeling, an emotion. It became a challenge to attempt to peel back someone's layers, paying particular attention to the slant of someone's eyes or the curl of their lip.

Although I was getting better at art, art was not encouraged by my parents or my teachers. I was a straight-A student and an athlete with scholarship offers to many schools, but my parents did not think college was necessary, refusing to send in my applications, and my teachers thought art was a waste of my intelligence. Therefore, I graduated high school unsure of what I would do, but with my sights still focused on a creative job. That job would come in the form of climbing and painting billboards for a sign shop in North Philadelphia. My parents would never know I was one hundred feet in the air painting, for fear they wouldn't allow it. In the next five years, I'd get married, have twins, and move to Florida where I'd start the therapy I spoke of earlier.

As my kids grew, I drew them. I was getting better and better, experimenting with different materials like chalk and paint. I started showing my artwork in shows organized by local art organizations and I developed a series of portraits called "INK" Women and Their Tattoos. This was considered an interesting subject matter since tattoos weren't common or deemed socially acceptable on females yet. Anywhere I was if I spotted a female with tattoos I'd chase them down and ask if I could paint them. Thank god it wasn't long before they were chasing me down asking if I'd include them in my series, but I found myself wanting the series to be more than just women and their tattoos. I wanted to know more about them, more about how we the public viewed the women, and how they viewed themselves. After showing the series in forty-five different venues, from group art shows to restaurants and bars to hair salons, finally, a gallery chose to represent me. As an artist, representation from a gallery was everything. In the art world, it meant you had made it, in the real world it meant you no longer stored your paintings in the garage. I morphed my INK series into a series called Dare to Be Different and had my first solo show in May of 2014 at Gallery 2014 in Hollywood, Florida. My paintings consisted of mostly women and a few men. My artist statement read - "Through my own tug of war between self-expression and fitting in, I have stumbled upon a group of people who dared to be different. Intrigued by each individual's ability to celebrate self, I simply paint the people who affect me." A reporter from The New Times in South Florida would write after seeing the show, "The alluring expressions of the bold tatted and pierced alt-ladies in the portraits convey strength and confidence- with just a hint of vulnerability." During the opening, I observed an elderly woman standing just inches from one of my paintings, carefully examining the detailed tattoos that spread across the arms of a painted bride in her bridal gown. After what must have been at least five minutes, she broke her gaze, turned and approached me saying "These women are so beautiful. I'm not sure I would have ever stopped long enough to really notice that, had you not painted them." That statement would change the trajectory of my art career. I would realize my artwork could communicate a message without me having to say a word. I wasn't sure yet what the message would be, but I knew this was an opportunity to make a difference.

Five months later on a Saturday night, I was attending a screening of a movie called, *Girl Rising*. It was a fundraiser for an organization by the same name. The movie would tell the story of nine young girls, all who had huge life obstacles and challenges to face, yet managed to find the determination and courage to prevail. *Girl Rising's* focus was to raise awareness around human trafficking and also the importance of educating a girl. The stories were all moving, but one story affected me like none of the others. It was of a seven-year-old girl named Wadley. Wadley had just survived the devastating 2010 earthquakes in Haiti. She was living now with her mother in a tent camp. The world around her was in pieces; many of which seemed beyond repair. One day while fetching water for her mother she noticed a school being taught in a nearby tent. Wadley loved school, so she put down her bucket and sat on the bench with the other students. The teacher spotted her and asked if her mother had paid for the school. Wadley said no, they had no money so she was asked to leave. The next day as Wadley was walking and noticing the devastation around her, she thought to herself, if I am here, if I survived, surely I must be special! So Wadley went back to the school and sat on the bench with the other kids. Again she was asked, "has your mother paid?" And was told she must leave. Wadley turned to the teacher and said, "You can make me leave every day, but I will keep coming back. I will come back until you let me stay." The teacher, taken aback by the determined seven-year old finally gave into Wadley's resolve and allowed her to stay. This story went through every cell of my body, awakening me to that seven-year-old I used to be. The little girl with no fear, who knew she was meant for way bigger things than what was expected of her or what her environment was dictating. The next morning, I woke and wrote a business plan for *Girl Noticed.* A non-profit that would travel to all fifty states recognizing girls and women who were nominated from their communities to be noticed. Large charcoal murals would be created of the girls and women nominated and they would fade off the wall with the message "Notice Me" in big letters. I would urge communities to "notice" before the very things that these girls and women value in themselves fade away or disappears completely. Through my artwork I thought, if I could inspire just one girl to hold onto the belief they had in themselves I'd have succeeded. I believed I could also empower girls and women who hadn't yet realized their value. It took me about five hours to conceptualize the entire project, and I had not one ounce of doubt that it was what I was supposed to be doing. Immediately I started moving forward.

My first plan of action was to show my idea to three people. The first was my closest friend and biggest cheerleader. I knew she'd be excited, tell me it was amazing, and say go for it. The second was another very good friend who I knew would tear the plan apart and tell me everything that was wrong with it. She's practical and a critical thinker. I figured it was best I knew the issues and problems upfront. So I listened intently as she told me all the things wrong with my plan. No one would fund temporary murals. How would I get other states to recognize the project? Never mind that I had never done a mural in charcoal. I nodded my head, said thank you, and moved on to the third person. The owner of the gallery that was representing me. I was beyond nervous. We had grown close and I really respected her opinion. I also felt she needed to know the direction I wanted to take my art. I dressed up in business attire, which was a far stretch from my normal attire of paint-splattered jeans, sneakers, and a t-shirt. I made an appointment instead of just dropping in so that we wouldn't be interrupted and body trembling sat across the table and handed her a typed plan and description of *Girl Noticed.* She carefully read through each page, closed my folder and asked if she could travel with me as the photographer I had described in detail in the plan. She would turn out to be incredibly supportive and umbrella me under her own non-profit, helping me to fundraise and get things off the ground. After just two years, *Girl Noticed* had been to 5 states, I had completed several murals, and was featured in Marie Claire magazine. I was at the height of my artistic career, being recognized for my art, but would learn height is somewhat of an illusion and what seemed like a personal high turned out to be my lowest low. In hindsight, I believe it was because I was still living my life as though it was me against all odds, and I always had something to prove, especially to myself. I was broke. I was alone, and my best friend was a bottle of vodka, which quickly became my worst enemy when it was empty. I was in Lincoln, Nebraska speaking at a bookstore about the mural I'd be painting the next day when I'd hear the words coming out of my mouth. "Believe in yourself, you matter, you have value." I met the gaze of a teenage girl with wide eyes soaking in every word I said, and I realized what a hypocrite I had become. I wasn't living my life like I had value. I didn't even like myself and I certainly wasn't an example anyone should follow.

Things had to change and I needed the help of others. I needed to put aside what I thought I knew and listen to the suggestions of others. I also had to accept my judgment wasn't always the best in those beginning years of my non-profit. Trust had been severed and I was left in a place where financially I had no control over the money I had raised. I had also lost support where I had wanted to advance with *Girl Noticed* as an organization. I would not allow this to be the end of *Girl Noticed.* I had witnessed the pride and empowerment my murals could bring to not only the girls and women I was painting, but their families and their communities. I was thrilled with the attention it brought to the organizations I worked with and how the murals often highlighted such important causes that so many of the girls and women represented. I mapped out a plan, and I broke that plan up into its smallest pieces so that every day I could get something done. I got incredibly clear on *Girl Noticed's* purpose by writing out my intentions for the project. Daily I reached out to whoever would listen and explained the mission of *Girl Noticed.* I read countless books about non-profits, productivity, and purpose. I read biographies by women who had empowered themselves and overcome every obstacle. I listened to daily YouTube videos on motivation and Oprah's Super Soul Conversations would play in my headphones while I painted. I stayed away from drama that would drag me down, whether on social media or television. I kept myself focused and moving. I made myself ready for any opportunity that presented itself to me and was clear on which ones were truly opportunities and which would likely become burdens. I learned how to be a leader by leading and being led, and in 2019 became my own 501C3. I developed workshops, awarded scholarships, and became comfortable speaking so I could make the *Girl*

Noticed experience one that could have a greater impact on the communities I served. It's been five and a half years since I saw the *Girl Rising* film, and I've been to fifteen states, created thirty-eight murals, held dozens of workshops and awarded two scholarships. Some days I still feel like I haven't done nearly enough, but that only drives me to do more.

Today my seven-year-old self walks alongside me. I imagine her holding Wadley's hand and we smile with our heads held high. There is not a girl that will cross our path that won't know she is uniquely special and beautiful.

Personal Reflections/Notes
Nonprofit Wisdom & Insights

_____

_____

_____

_____

_____

_____

_____

_____

_____

_____

_____

_____

Personal Reflections/Notes
Nonprofit Wisdom & Insights

Author Rhonika Thomas

Author Rhonika Thomas

Rhonika Thomas, (Dr. Rho) is considered a pioneer in the nonprofit sector and created history as the CEO and Founder of the first National Nonprofit Minority Association in the world. Born and raised in St. Louis, Missouri, her educational background is solid with the following degrees, BA, MA, and Ph.D. She is considered an expert in the field of nonprofit development and management. She has spent years dedicating her time to learning about nonprofits. Her love and passion have taken her across the world coaching and developing future nonprofit leaders. Dr. Rho created the first online Facebook group entitled Blacks in Nonprofits. This community is open to African Americans all across the world and is growing rapidly. Her mission in life is to help others to reach their full potential and give back to her community. She believes in being a blessing to others. She established Nonprofit Newbies Consulting, LLC based out of St. Louis, Missouri and founded the Phenomenal I am Women's Conference series that provides encouragement, empowerment, and networking opportunities for women of all backgrounds. However, her proudest accomplishment is becoming a proud and loving mother to three amazing children who she proudly declares are her reasons why she goes so hard in life.

Don't Count Yourself Out

There are over 7.5 billion people on earth. The great and amazing thing about that is there is absolutely no one else like you. The journey to start your nonprofit, I found out through experience, is very similar to this. There are over 1.56 million nonprofits registered with the Internal Revenue Service (IRS). No matter how many nonprofits are created daily, monthly, or yearly, the one you created is unique and special with its own identity that you give it.

Starting a nonprofit can be scary and a hard decision to make for anyone debating if it is the right decision for them or not. Trust me; I know. I was once in those same shoes and feeling a mixture of being nervous and scared at the same time. This was 12 years ago, but I remember it like it was yesterday. For me, my nonprofit legacy began as a single mom of three, working a full time job, going to school full time to finish my Doctoral degree, and establishing a nonprofit. Talk about wearing multiple hats, I was mastering all of those roles as an eager and passionate woman out to do good in my community. At least so I thought. Everyone told me all the great things that came from starting a nonprofit, but I was left completely blindsided by all the rest that comes with it.

So now, as I look back on my journey and reflect on what words I wished someone would have said to me, I am giving them to you as my six principles of nonprofit growth and development. I wish someone experienced in the nonprofit sector would have shared these guidelines with me. No matter if you are just starting out or have had your nonprofit for years, these six principles can be directly applied to wherever you are in life.

Principle 1-Don't Count Yourself Out

You will be surprised at the number of people that count themselves out of jobs, promotions, relationships, cars, houses, and happiness due to feeling as if they are not worthy of good things for themselves. We get into a nasty habit of settling for less than what we deserve and putting limits on our possibilities. How many times have you found yourself guilty of talking yourself out of something that would have been great for you or that you felt like you didn't deserve? How did that make you feel? If you are anything like me, it made you feel horrible. There came a point in my life when I decided that I would never deny what my possibilities were and where they could take me. I recall several people discouraging me from starting my nonprofit because it was an idea that had never been done before. I quickly found myself questioning my abilities to bring my vision to life because I allowed the fear of others to become my own. So before I knew it I had counted myself out of starting a nonprofit due to lack of confidence in my own abilities and lack of belief in the power of counting myself *in* as a potential executive director. Why? You may wonder. Well, simply put, I counted myself out before I even gave myself a shot at it. As you continue reading on, you will quickly understand why your mental approach to everything in life is so important.

Repeat this: Don't count yourself out; never deny what your possibilities can do and where they can take you. The first step in doing anything in life is the belief that you can!!!

Principle 2- You are Allowed to be Great in Your Space

Once you believe that you can do what it is you set out to achieve, the battle shifts outwards. The world is an impressive place filled with lots of good things and good people, but it is also filled with the bad. Learning how to maneuver through both sides can be challenging for the best of the best. It is how you respond to the events and things in your life that will determine your outcomes. You are a very powerful individual and have control over your thoughts and actions. Just think, what would have occurred if I had listened to the naysayers, aka haters who tried to talk me out of starting my nonprofit because it was a foreign concept to them. I would be beating myself up to this day with all the *what if's, coulda's* and *shoulda's* of what could have been. I realized that I had the power to be great in my own space and that changed the game for me. I hope that by reading this, it now changes the game for you as well. It is a liberating feeling to know that you are capable of achieving great things and you will. Never allow anyone to shrink your ability; to keep you contained in a box. If you go through life depending on others' reality of you and not your own, you will always fall short of experiencing the power of the unknown. So allow yourself to be great in your space and dare to be different. As you probably guessed, it is "yes", I pushed past the naysayers and started my very first nonprofit as a single mom of three, a Doctoral student, and a full time employee.

Principle 3- Say Yes to God

So I'm not even going to try and sugar coat it, I'm nothing and I do mean nothing, without God!! I have tried to do many things without Him and learned the hard way that you need Him to succeed. You can experience success without Him. However, after a while, you will start to crave that longevity success that is obtained by saying "yes" to God. The days as an Executive Director of your own nonprofit or someone else's can be tough and frustrating. Not to mention the feelings of being overwhelmed, stressed, and experiencing anxiety can really take a toll on you mentally and physically. There have been days when I seriously questioned if the nonprofit sector was the right field for me. Have you ever questioned if this field was right for you? If you answered "yes", welcome to what I call "the unsure phase". During this phase, you begin to question everything!!! Did I name it the right thing? Am I going to raise any money to do this? How in the world am I going to pull this off? Omg, it costs how much to become a 501c3? What do you mean I need a board? Then you finally come to the determination that maybe this is a bit too much and maybe not for you. No worries, we have all been there before and some of us visit that unsure phase weekly, heck sometimes-daily lol. The important thing to remember is that with God, all things are possible and with Him you can do whatever your heart desires, including running a successful nonprofit. If you trust Him with everything else, why not put your nonprofit in his hands, too. This will require you trusting that He will bring the right people to help you, He will open doors that man can't and be with you every step of the way if you just say "yes" to Him. I did, and my nonprofit was tremendously blessed because I included God and trusted him through the process. So remember when in doubt, trust God to see you through the unsure phase no matter how often it may visit you.

Principle 4- Create Your Opportunity

Life is not always going to hand you a fresh-squeezed lemonade. Sometimes you have to grab your own lemons and squeeze them yourself and make your own darn glass!!! My nonprofit was now legally established and registered with the state. I was on cloud 9 and feeling very ecstatic about my newly formed nonprofit as many brand new nonprofit founders are. Do you remember how you felt when you first received the news that your organization was approved for its tax-exempt status? If you have not reached that point yet, keep going because when you do, it will be an awesome feeling indeed. Stepping out into the nonprofit sector has been a bit overwhelming, so I highly recommend getting a mentor or a consultant that can walk you through the "what's next phase" you immediately jump into after you realize you are now legally committed to implementing your nonprofit. I was extremely lucky to have an amazing mentor that helped guide me through the beginning and her insight was priceless. It is important to find someone that truly cares about you and that stands behind your mission. The unfortunate part was the nonprofit I established was a concept never done before, so her level of expertise could only carry me to a specific point. I quickly found myself in charge of creating my own opportunity. Some people's stomachs start to turn just at the thought of trying to figure out how to do something new with no directions, but not mine. As a little child, my mother often told me that I was very independent and loved to do things for myself. This most definitely carried over to adulthood because I am always challenging myself to be a pioneer. I love creating things that are a first and making my own path as I go. I learned that if an opportunity is not there, it's the perfect time to create your own. Please keep in mind again, there are millions of nonprofits across the world and some are doing the same thing in a different city, state, or even country. However, that does not mean the work you will be doing is not needed in *your* community. If there are similar nonprofits in your city doing the same mission you would like to do, it may be best to partner with them to make a bigger impact. If you are like me and there is not a nonprofit like yours, do not be afraid to create the change you wish to see.

Principle 5- Take Action on Your Faith

So here I find myself all in with my nonprofit. My family and friends all know about it and are willing to support it. I created the Facebook page for my nonprofit and had a beautiful website created. I signed up for all the free nonprofit workshops, seminars, and webinars I could find to educate myself on my new adventure in what I nicknamed *nonprofithood*. I went to the library and checked out book after book on everything you could think of that related to nonprofits because I didn't want to miss a thing. When you are just starting out, your energy level is off the chain lol, but you eventually slow down and find a rhythm of learning that works best for you. There is so much to know. I found it helpful to break it down into categories and learn a little in each category over a span of time versus bombarding myself with too much information all at once. The important thing I did was not sit idle. It is crucial that you take action steps once you step out on faith and start your nonprofit. Taking action is what is going to keep you motivated on your journey. Action is what is going to keep you excited to do events, to serve your population with enthusiasm, to keep going on the days that you feel like you don't want to. I believe that throughout this journey, staying active and involved in the community has definitely inspired me to keep going.

There were several doors closed in my face, more no's than yes's, sometimes nobody showed up, other times there was standing room only. Sometimes I didn't have a dime in the nonprofit bank account and didn't know how to change that. Other times donations would pour in like a flood. The point of it all is that you don't know what your nonprofit journey will bring when you first start off. God knows I sure didn't, but once I learned how to change my mentality to a winning attitude and determined nothing would stop me, achieving my goals became easier. I hope you too, can come to these terms and continue to strive for greatness. Once I started taking those action steps, I never stopped stepping. Before I knew it, people were contacting me to volunteer for my organization, contacting me to be spotlighted on the news for the work I was doing with my nonprofit. Last but certainly not least, the donations were coming in on a monthly basis. I found myself loving every minute of it. Did this happen overnight? No, we have been progressing forward in my journey. It has been in the last few years that I had my nonprofit, that all these amazing things occurred. The 12-year ride with my first nonprofit was an incredible experience filled with overflowing joy and passion for the thousands of children it served. I had the privilege of taking my mission internationally, over to Nigeria and blessing children there as well. I believe all of my experiences with my first nonprofit lead and prepared me for the nonprofit I have now.

Principle 6: When you are a blessing to others God turns around and blesses you

I truly believe with all my heart and soul that when you are a blessing to others, God will turn right around and find a way to bless you. I adopted that as my motto a few years ago and it has stuck with me ever since. Everyone's nonprofit journey will be different and no one can tell your personal story better than you. I have been blessed beyond my biggest dreams and because I have, I knew God was directing me for an even larger role. All the leadership courses, all the webinars, seminars, books, YouTube videos, and training I did over the years were all for my greater good. It's funny how when you are going through the storms of life, you never really stop and think how God may be using those very storms to mold and shape you into the future version of yourself he can use to bless his people. Sometimes you can have all the skills, gifts, and talents on the inside of you, but they are not crafted enough to be brought out yet. I know so much more now about the nonprofit sector as I am beginning my second nonprofit than I knew during my first.

The principles we discussed are all things you can take and directly apply to your life and nonprofit today. Always remember: (1) never count yourself out or ever deny what your possibilities can do and take you. (2) you are allowed to be great in your space. (3) always say "yes" to God. (4) create your opportunity. (5) take action on your faith. and (6) when you are a blessing to others, God will bless you.

Personal Reflections/Notes
Nonprofit Wisdom & Insights

_____

_____

_____

_____

_____

_____

_____

_____

_____

_____

_____

_____

Personal Reflections/Notes
Nonprofit Wisdom & Insights

Author Sandy Washington

Author Sandy Washington

Mrs. Sandy Washington has worked and lived in the Southern Maryland community for over 35 years addressing its needs. In 1998, she co-founded **LifeStyles of Maryland Foundation, Inc.**, whose mission is to empower people and assist in providing a better quality of life through social awareness and community development. Although the organization is located in La Plata, Maryland, they provide assistance to residents throughout Southern Maryland and developed a model of service delivery that has been replicated in several states. Mrs. Washington and the organization have been recognized throughout the State of Maryland for their dedication to serving those who are homeless. **LifeStyles** was named the Nonprofit of the year by the Charles County Chamber of Commerce and the local newspaper, the Maryland Independent. From street outreach to more permanent housing initiatives, the organization serves over 14,000 people annually. In 2018, the organization developed **The Market,** a business focused on getting farm-fresh food to food deserts in rural Southern Maryland. In 2019, **Southern Crossing, LLC** was formed. This six-acre property, which was a vacant motel, is being transformed to twenty-seven apartments that will house seventy-seven low-income individuals.

Mrs. Sandy Washington is the Vice-President of the Maples Foundation and the Maples Limited Liability Corp., which provides affordable senior housing for over 93 senior citizens in Charles County. She is also the Vice Chair of the Dorchester Community Center, serving a low-income community and serves on the Board of Directors for End Hunger in Charles County focusing on food-insecure families and Real Women, Inc. an international organization offering a safe place for women to express themselves. Her knowledge of organizational development allowed her to develop the Regional Alzheimer's office in Southern Maryland, before establishing **LifeStyles.** All of these organizations collectively work together to provide the necessary services and programs that residents need to improve their quality of life and well-being.

Mrs. Washington has received several gubernatorial appointments that include the Judicial Nominating Committee and Medical Cannabis Commission. Just recently, she was appointed for a four-year term to Governor Hogan's newly formed Maryland Efficient Grant Application Council. She also has received: Woman of the Year, Charles County Commission for Women Trailblazer Award, and Congressional Recognition as an exceptional Business. Mrs. Washington is a Paul Harris Fellow, a Kiwanian and was inducted into the Community Foundation of Southern Maryland's Philanthropy Hall of Fame. For years she has received numerous citations, awards and recognition from law enforcement, Charles County State's Attorney and a myriad of businesses, organizations, and agencies. She works closely with the local and state government agencies and community organizations.

During her local, state, and federal committee appointments, Mrs. Washington has stayed close to the community and brings to the forefront the needs of the community with a special place in her heart for the elderly and children.

Don't Eat Your Seed

L et me begin by saying my journey has been a faith walk. While many may have inspired, mentored, and poured into me, this walk has been and is personal. It is between me and God and He continually reminds me because I continually ask Him. The thing about a faith walk is no one can take it for you. Your tolerance for pain, heartbreak, disappointment, and endurance is individually measured, meaning it is different for each person.

My faith and sometimes lack thereof has been tested throughout this journey. I sometimes wonder where it came from: this strong belief in God. I did not come from a particularly religious family. Maybe it came from a need to call on someone greater than myself as I navigated through a tumultuous childhood. A childhood wrought with days without food, foster care, and making up stories so the neighbors would not report us to child welfare. As the eldest of seven, I learned early how to care for others. It was not until much later in life that I realized caring and service to others was my gift.

This led me to something much larger than I could ever imagine, the creation of a non-profit organization that would be known as **LifeStyles of Maryland.** Later, the establishment of two other companies, **Southern Crossing, LLC** - a twenty-seven apartment complex that will house seventy-seven low-income families and **The Market, LLC.** , a mobile healthy food initiative distributing farm-fresh food to isolated locations throughout rural communities in Southern Maryland.

I imagine most have heard the story of Jonah and his time in the whale. Well, my journey was a little like his: going everywhere but where I was supposed to go. Like Jonah in the belly of the whale, when you finally get to your Nineveh you wonder why you took so many detours and stops on the way to your destiny. I tried so many safe ways to do what I thought God wanted me to do. The ability to still collect a paycheck while helping others sounds good and works for many, but I needed to trust Him with everything. Now I am not telling anyone to quit your *day job* as they say. You'll know when it's time. I just couldn't serve God and someone else anymore. That was my personal faith walk, I tried securing and maintaining contracts and taking opportunities offered to make sure I had an income that folks would understand; mainly my husband. How do you explain that you are walking away from a salary that can pay your bills to, "I don't know, I'm just listening to God"? Sometimes I wonder- "Is this what Noah felt as he built the ark or what others that just stepped out on faith felt?" At this point, I was conflicted and I couldn't fully commit to these contracts that would allow me to do this non-profit thing without question. Day One in the whale: I could really do what God wanted me to do if I connected with others or with another organization that would offer me some safety. Day Two in the whale: No matter how successful I was at any of those ventures, nothing felt right. I still saw people suffering, unable to find shelter, food resources for their children or employment. I saw people without hopes or dreams. Day Three in the whale: Finally, I told God I was ready! Welcome to Nineveh.

Over twenty-five years ago, when God gave me the vision which I shared with a friend who was willing to connect her faith with mine, we created *LifeStyles.* There was not a pool of resources available giving all the advice on how to start a non-profit and information on boards and suggested guidelines. I should say I did not know where to look for that information. Much of what was learned in the early years came from trial and error, mostly error. The lessons that I learned were costly and probably taught me more than I could ever gain in any classroom. These lessons were like fire. Once you get burnt, no one ever has to tell you not to put your hands there again. I remember the first grant we received for $250 from the local health department. I was so excited to think a government agency would entrust us enough to give us money to do what we loved doing.

I remember a wise mentor telling me that private money follows government money. Well, I knew we were well on our way. Our first year ended with a three-person volunteer staff having assisted over eight hundred people and a net income of a whopping fifty-seven dollars. Twenty-five years later, we serve about 15,000 people annually, have six million in assets, 3 million in real estate, two million plus operating budget, thirty staff and two thousand volunteers. I believe this is a result of compassionate people passionately serving one person at a time as if it were their own family needing help.

All that I have gone through in my life has prepared me for such a time as this. Each experience has given me the tools needed to succeed or survive failure. I have learned from all the people who have crossed my path. I made the decision whether to emulate them or not. Every encounter is meant to be a learning experience or a teachable moment. I looked for any organization that was doing anything like what I envisioned. I truly couldn't find one that did all of the things I was thinking of and really, I didn't even know all the areas I would cover. But I had a willingness to serve and an eagerness to learn. When you follow your heart and mind and you walk into your destiny, boy does it feel right. It is not easy but it's good. Every step led me to the next. It was like the Indiana Jones movie where he had to get to the other side of this cave, and it looked as if there was a bottomless pit he had to cross. Well, every time he placed his foot down there was ground. That was me every time. When I kept my eyes on serving and showing the people we served that we cared, there was always solid ground. With that in mind my passion grew. Each person helped just fanned the flames.

I remember the first-time walking through the woods going to a homeless encampment to check on a gentleman. It was the dead of winter and you could see items discarded where people had dumped trash. I thought God, look we've thrown away people just like we've thrown away all these things. When I saw how these folks were living and some not complaining, I knew God had prepared me for such a time as this. Our organization began to advocate for folks that people just didn't think existed. Soon we became known for caring for the homeless and disadvantaged in this rural community in Southern Maryland. We had found our niche. A voice for the voiceless. Making people look at areas of their community that they didn't know or want to know existed. We began to find our own way to serve this population, built on trust and compassion. We started implementing programs that had not been introduced to our community and soon people were asking us to do more and reach families that they hadn't been able to reach. What is interesting is that as I inquired of other larger organizations regarding funding and program models, I found people were not eager to share. Since the inception of **LifeStyles, Inc.**, I have been willing to share anything that could make it easier for the next person. Mainly because I believe that No one can take what God means for me. And I believe that He has so much for me that if I don't share it I couldn't possibly hold it all. There is a balance between sharing an idea that you have not put in place and sharing information or experiences or resources. Many times, people take an idea not yet realized and implement it in a manner it was not meant to be. This can have a negative effect when you come back and try to implement it in the right way. The right ideas implemented by the wrong people could hamper its acceptance. I've also learned not to be upset when you share your dreams and people don't get it. Don't force it. They are not supposed to get it. God gave it to you for such a time as this.

As you have probably gathered, I do an awful lot of praying. One of my constant prayers has been to remember. "Lord when you provide what I asked for, help me to remember what I said I would do if you gave it to me." This may sound silly, but I can remember praying for money to take care of a bill. Well, the money came and went, and the bill was still there. So, when I began to pray the same thing, I realized that when my prayers were answered I didn't even think about that bill. From then on, I prayed to remember and follow through. As the organization grew and we increased our donors and started diversifying funding streams, I could not understand why we did not have the needed cash flow. Again, God placed on my heart "stop eating your seed". For seeds to grow you must nurture the soil, plant the seed, and water as needed. I found ways after this revelation to sow into other people's dreams, ideas, and organizations. 10% of every dollar we take in goes to our reserve and 10% is sown. So far, our seeds have grown into real estate and other assets and organizations helping people in areas that we don't have an expertise in.

I believe as we continue to grow and learn, my desire is to fill the gaps that keep the underserved from living a full, happy, and healthy life. How we do this may change as the needs of the population changes. While I have spoken of our financial success, although minimal as compared to many other non-profits and the notoriety gained through successful service, I have a final test. It is the test to walk away. I believe God put me on this path to serve. Ultimately to serve Him by serving His people. If I get star-struck by the accolades or think more highly of myself than I ought to. I could lose sight of why I do what I do and for who. So, my test is, what if God said, "Sandy walk away now". Would I come up with excuses as to why I couldn't? If so, then I'm no longer doing any of this for Him and my entire story would change.

Personal Reflections/Notes
Nonprofit Wisdom & Insights

_____

_____

_____

_____

_____

_____

_____

_____

_____

_____

_____

_____

Author Sharon Anderson

Author Sharon Anderson

Raised in Suitland, Maryland, Sharon Anderson is a proud alumnus of Suitland High School. In 2007, she completed her studies at Prince George's Community College where she graduated with honors and received an Associates in Marketing Management degree. In May 2009, she completed her Bachelor of Arts degree in Business Management at the College of Notre Dame (Baltimore, MD), after returning from Taiwan where she studied aboard at Providence University.

Sharon has worked with area youth for more than 20 years. Sharon volunteered as a mentor to youth in the Prince George's County Department of Social Services Foster Care System. This ultimately led her to become the instructor for its Independent Living Program. Sharon taught life skills to adolescent youth transitioning out of the foster care. Having a strong passion for mentoring and educating the youth, especially young women, she has also worked within her church and with other non-profits, community, and state organizations. Sharon has received several awards for her youth empowerment efforts.

Today, she is the founder and executive director of *Girl Speak Inc.* a non-profit organization founded in 2014 in the Washington, DC Metropolitan area. *Girl Speak Inc.* kicked off its official launch/fundraiser during Women's History Month in March 2016. Partnering with the Suitland Civic Association and M-NCPPC, she created *Girl Speak's* signature program, "How's your S.E.L.F.I.E. game?" that received recognition from the local area school board.

Ms. Anderson is the proud mother of one daughter and resides in Suitland, Maryland.

She Believed She Could, So She Did!

The first time I came across the quote *"She believed she could so she did."* I was working part-time at the local Hallmark store. It struck a chord with me as this small green canvas sign stood out like a flashing bright light on the store shelf, as I set up a display. That statement seemed to define how I had chosen to live my life; now I had found something that truly articulated my philosophy. I, a teen mom at 16, disliked the social stigma and associated stereotypes and labels placed on young unmarried mothers. Especially those that indicated these young women would ultimately remain uneducated and unsuccessful. I promised myself I would not conform to these statistics of failure, but create a narrative of determination. My life was dedicated to raising and being an example to my college-bound daughter. It had not been easy, but I was on the road to accomplishing my goal.

I was now 40-something, just returning from Florida after successfully completing the Walt Disney World College Program. Not only had I decided I would complete my undergraduate degree, but I was going to live on campus while I did it. The College of Notre Dame was a small private women's college nestled in a suburban residential area in Baltimore County, Maryland. My arrival, as its first adult student living on campus, caused a certain level of excitement. The maturated students usually attended their evening courses and participated in campus life on a limited basis, but for the next three years, I would live the life of a traditional student. My adventurousness would lead other women to do the same.

I applied for the resident assistant position when I became eligible and was selected for the next school term. During my first year as an RA, I was assigned to the senior dorm and was recognized as the *RA of the Year*. During my senior year, the college accepted an influx of freshmen who were the first in their families to attend college. This freshmen class required consistent attention, often clashing with the assigned RA who was merely a year or two older than they were. While I was away in Taiwan completing my study abroad semester, I received a call from the Vice President of Student Affairs asking me to accept the RA reassignment to the freshmen dorm when I returned. She explained she thought I could be helpful to these young ladies as I had life experiences that they could benefit from. This meant I would have to move into the freshmen dorm, a building without any air conditioning, however, I would receive two rooms with a bathroom connecting them. I set up one room as my personal living quarters and the other, a colorful space full of affirmations and fun trinkets where I could talk with the girls or they could hang out.

As I became acquainted with the freshman class, I saw a diverse group of young ladies. Any one of them could have been my daughter. They were all in need of the same things - encouragement, confidence building, and discipline. I decided it would be helpful if they had a place to be heard and a place to hear wise counsel. I decided to create an outlet giving them the opportunity to talk and discuss any issues affecting their daily lives. I called the session *Girl Speak.*

How I Got to *Girl Speak*

In the beginning, I was just trying to survive the sole responsibilities of parenting as a determined single teen mom. Translation: obtain full-time employment while attending community college part-time to provide my daughter with greater educational and social-economic opportunities. But it became an evolution of who I was and who I was becoming, which eventually led me to my purpose. Long before I reached the College of Notre Dame campus or participated in the Walt Disney World College Program, the seeds of forming a non-profit were planted without me realizing it. I volunteered as a mentor to youth in the county's Department of Social Services Foster Care System and received an *Outstanding Service* Award. This led me to become the instructor for its Independent Living Program teaching life skills to adolescent youth transitioning out of foster care.

I had successfully built a career at a company where I had worked for ten years. I left there for what I thought would be an opportunity of a lifetime to work with a mentor and former manager on an international venture, which was suspended indefinitely. This unfortunately was the start of a period of irregular employment that lasted more than ten years.

Although I had the work experience required for such management jobs, I didn't have the educational requirements. The continuous employment denials affected my confidence and belief that I would be gainfully employed again, but I couldn't sit in a corner and feel sorry for myself. I still had a daughter to raise.

Throughout periods of un- and under-employment, working short term contracts and temporary assignments, I never gave up my youth-related efforts. With the support of my church, I developed and coordinated my first one-day conference for girls entitled *Star Potential*, attended by over 75 young ladies, ages 9 to 23, and a subsequent forum, *Where Have All The Good Girls Gone: A Self Examination and Discovery on Rejection.*

Unemployed once again, it was now five years later, and I hadn't had permanent employment. I realized it was time to complete my education. I returned to community college as a full-time student and worked in the Dean of Student Affairs office. I interviewed and was accepted into the WDW College Program. I left for Orlando, FL, that winter and interned at the Magic Kingdom's Emporium for the next seven months, where I received a *Great Service Fanatic Award* and attended the renowned Disney University. Known as "Mama Sharon" around the Emporium, I was always giving advice, especially to the young people I worked with.

Upon returning to the Washington DC metro area, I enrolled at the College of Notre Dame. I transferred the credits from CND to Prince George's Community College for the last two courses needed to complete my degree. After more than 20 years of attending school part-time, in 2007, I graduate with honors and received. my Associates in Marketing Management degree. In 2009, I graduated from Notre Dame with a B.A. in Business Management.

The evolution of my "becoming" was realized through my life experiences in preparation to fulfill my purpose of youth empowerment. Living the life of a traditional college student as an adult had uniquely given me an uncommon perspective and insight. The girl programs I had created on star potential and handling rejection hadn't been just for them only; I too benefited from the lessons learned. I was one of those girls that I was trying to reach. It had shown me that confidence and self-assurance are often the difference between conquerors and the conquered in any circumstance. Preparation made all the difference. Despite remaining active as a church youth leader and scholarship president, I had always imagined creating a youth development program, especially for girls ensuring they have the tools to make good decisions and live as productive individuals.

During this period, I was working with a Christian life coach who had become a mentor and a friend, I called her Dr. P. She encouraged me to take the time to hear from God about my purpose. Prayerfully, I penned my thoughts that would outline the foundation for my assignment. I called it *B.L.I.N.G. - Boldly Living IN God.* Dr. P. assigned me to begin the implementation of B.L.I.N.G., and I started to research funding and grant information. Although I was continuously prayerful; a lack of satisfaction still overshadowed what I had developed. As I was praying about it alone one evening, I heard a voice telling me repeatedly *"**girl speak**".* I began to pray out loud. As I did I felt I was reclaiming my "voice" lost from the stigma of being a 16-year-old unwed teen mother, lost from the repeated employment rejections because I didn't have a degree and from any life experience in which my voice had been diminished. My assignment had become completely clear; I was to empower young ladies to "live life out loud" and use positive lifestyle choices as a "voice" to express who they are. I immediately changed the name to *Girl Speak.*

I never planned to start a non-profit. I was simply looking for a grant writer to obtain funding when I met LaSandra, my consultant. She was a referral from a friend. As I talked with her about my vision and all I desired to do, she asked me to consider establishing a 501c3 non-profit organization, believing my purpose was bigger than what I envisioned. Once I mentally committed to starting a non-profit, I thought of the movie, *First Wives Clubs,* starring Goldie Hawn, Diane Keaton, and Bette Milder. After meeting again at the funeral of their college friend who committed suicide because her husband left her, the trio of ex-wives seek revenge against their ex-husbands. Ultimately, they realize their goal should be greater and decide to establish a center for women using an old abandon warehouse. In the final minutes of the movie, they invite the community and host a lavish grand opening of the building so beautifully decorated. I dream of owning such a building someday to benefit the girls and the community.

Before I formally confirmed working with LaSandra to obtain the federal tax exemption status, I committed myself to the financial requirements, whatever the costs. Working with her turned out to be one of the best investments of time, energy, and money I made in helping with this non-profit development process. LaSandra guided me through each step, up to the launch; the many hours of guidance, direction, and professional tidbits she gave me were invaluable.

After the excitement of receiving my tax exemption status letter subsided, the reality of what was ahead set in. I needed an image that would come to mind every time someone heard about *Girl Speak*; I needed a logo. Who better to create our logo concept than a young female artist? Delighted, the artist presented a vibrant colored silhouette of a young lady's face with full lips emphasizing her mouth to represent a girl speaking. After a conversation with my pastor regarding the importance of branding and messaging, I needed to reconsider that decision to use the logo. A survey of several family members and friends asking for their impressions and thoughts confirmed my concerns. Everyone appreciated my attempt to use an artist from our target audience, but one answer was most surprising - the full lips in the girl's silhouette could be misconstrued as provocative. By no means was that the imagery I wanted to give. The logo design, created by a graphic designer recommended by my pastor, elevated the current concept to present a polished colorful image of a feminine silhouette that appealed to everyone and could be representative of any young lady.

We announced the forming of *Girl Speak Inc.* on Facebook 60 days before the launch and posted a couple of times a day to promote the organization and build a following. Held at a notable neighborhood art gallery, the inaugural celebration introduced *Girl Speak* as a creatively wonderful enrichment opportunity designed especially for young ladies; included musical and poetry performances, light hors'doeuvres and was attended by both the young and old. My pastor closed out the night with a spirited call for support and a prayer of dedication and blessings. LaSandra, holding my feet to the fire for the last 90 days to ensure I completed my startup checklist and preparations for the launch, paid off.

The success of the launch gave us momentum and garnered the attention of the genuinely interested and the curious. Having reached our financial goal, I wanted to demonstrate to our donors that their monetary gifts would be used to help young ladies as we promised. Our first event for the girls was a day-long conference entitled, *Image is Everything*. A popular local news anchor was our special guest and highlighted the event during her news segment the following Monday morning. The fees required by such personalities are usually more than a new non-profit could afford, but I wasn't deterred. I didn't ask her to appear for free but offered what was budgeted and she accepted. A former manager once told me, never be afraid to ask; you will be no worse off if the answer is no.

Almost five years since its launch, **Girl Speak** has created a signature life skills program and set up an office in the neighborhood community art center amongst the activities, workshops, and events created for the empowerment of our young ladies. It is equally rewarding to serve and impact the lives of others while also contributing to my evolution of becoming. Faith was and still is essential to my being. Despite my life challenges, I refused to stop believing. The formation of a nonprofit had not been my intended destination on my purpose journey. But it was that undiscovered spot I found, and I knew I had to invest in it.

I reflect on my decision to finish my degree – an investment in me. It wasn't enough to only take the courses, I needed the entire experience (i.e. living on campus, studying abroad) to fully realize its benefits. Like my education, **Girl Speak** too, is another one of the best investments I will ever make and requires the sum of "ME" to fulfill the mission. Always working in excellence to ensure that it remains a place of intention because the wisdom, insight, and preparation for **Girl Speak** began with me.

I believed I could, so I did!

Food for Thought:

- **It is a mindset** – be determined. Things will happen, events will occur that could cause you to lose focus, only if you let it.
- **Consider it an investment** – be prepared to spend some of your own money if necessary. Don't expect everything to be discounted or free. If you don't believe you are worth the investment, why should anyone else?
- **Get a business coach** – use their expertise to maximize your potential and effectiveness and to minimize avoidable pitfalls.
- **Run your non-profit organization like a for-profit business** – mistakenly non-profits aren't always managed with the same diligence as a for-profit business. A non-profit is still a business and requires the same level (sometimes more) discipline to be successful.
- **Do everything with excellence** – operate as if everything you do will lead you to your next opportunity. You never know who is watching you.
- **Don't be afraid to ask someone** – receipt of a negative response changes nothing, but if it is positive, new doors open and you benefit!

Personal Reflections/Notes
"I can't do BIG by myself."

Author Tajala Battle Lockhart

Visionary Author

Author Tajala Battle Lockhart

Mrs. Tajala "Taj" Lockhart is a Certified Hospitality Educator with a passion for training up our youth and young adults and coaching adults through adversity by providing-industry recognized certifications and training that provides them an opportunity to become successful independent citizens. Tajala is a newly-elected Governing Board Member for Charles County Board of Education, CEO of TAJ Consulting & Events, Founder/Executive Director of **Phenomenal Young Women, Inc.** a 501©3 Nonprofit, Best-Selling Author and Associate Professor for the Hospitality, Tourism & Culinary Arts Department at Prince George Community.

Tajala is a native of North Carolina but currently resides in Maryland with her husband and daughter. She graduated from Wake Technical Community College in 1998 with an Associate in Applied Science Degree in Hotel & Restaurant Management. In 2016, she obtained her Certified Hospitality Educator Certification recognized by the American Hotel & Lodging Association at Penn State University. She had a successful career in the Hospitality Industry for twenty-six years. Tajala now owns TAJ Consulting & Events which focuses on training and developing the workforce in the surrounding communities. She teaches other people how to achieve the same success through personal branding, understanding their *why*, and building strong interviewing skills and resumes. TAJ Consulting & Events trains up our future, coaches adults through adversity, and creates memorable events for clients.

This year, Tajala was awarded Entrepreneur & Women in Business, Nonprofit Star by National Nonprofit Minority Association. In 2019, she was awarded the My Sister's Keeper Award by The Sisterhood of Southern Maryland Organization, the ACHI Nonprofit Executive of the Year, nominated for ACHI Women of Achievement award, recognized as one of 16 Faces of Influence, received two Executive Citations from Anne Arundel County Executive 2019 & 2020, and was awarded Entrepreneur of the Year Nonprofit.

Embracing Your Resilience

As I reflect on my nonprofit journey, I have to take a step down memory lane, to where it all began. I started like most nonprofit leaders, I was all in with my whole heart and so much pain. I was ready to save all those little girls from feeling like I felt at a young age; lonely and with no one to really share my true feelings with. This was a personal pain that I carried for many years. Do not get me wrong, I grew up in a small town with my grandmother and it was truly the ole-school village for sure. Everyone supported each other and met the needs of anyone in the community. However, I struggled as a young girl wanting to have the best of all worlds. I wanted my mom, dad, grandma, and granddad. Unfortunately, my mom had me at 20 years old, and moved away, leaving me in North Carolina with my grandmother.

I never knew my father nor my grandfather. My uncles were the only real male relationships I had growing up. My mom and I had an in-and-out relationship until she finally moved back to North Carolina during my eighth grade year and I ended up living with her in Raleigh because my grandmother started to get sick more often. I was afraid to continue staying with her due to the fear of losing her to health issues. That lonely little girl with her complicated childhood experiences would leave a lasting imprint on me, one that I didn't realize would lead to the birth of my nonprofit until years later.

As we fast forward many years later, it was 2006 and I was blessed to become a mother. Now, it was my personal aim to provide to my child, all those things that I lacked growing up. My daughter, like me, is an only child. I feared her possibly ending up feeling like me, lonely. I truly did not want her to feel that at all, so I was committed to being a great wife to ensure that she had her dad in her life. Unfortunately, due to past family lies, I was unable to share her grandfather on my side of the family and a few years later, I lost my mother in 2012. I felt like all the things that I wanted to give her were disappearing before my eyes. In 2015, my daughter and I were involved in a lot of extracurricular activities and at one of the events we were attending, another mom approached me to ask if I would be interested in starting a nonprofit. I knew lots of work was required, but the idea had been on my mind. However, I did not feel that I could find people dedicated or committed enough to move forward with starting one. So, I did not move on the idea immediately. The following year, I met with that lady to continue our previous conversation, while researching everything that we needed to start our nonprofit. Through this legwork, we birthed **Phenomenal Young Women Inc.** on July 19, 2016. As we started our nonprofit journey, I realized that there was a great deal of information yet to learn.

We created an organization that would support young women holistically through Academics, Health & Wellness, Social Skills and Entrepreneurship. This allowed us to support them in every aspect of their lives. We were most excited to work with young women, teaching them the value of becoming and being a woman. We planned to support our group of girls by offering workshops, hosting events, and traveling to other youth events that were held by other organizations. We got off to a great start and got great exposure. The greatest challenge, at that time, was just finding a location that would allow us to meet consistently with our girls.

In the beginning, it did not hinder us very much but later, as the school year began, we were utilizing the local libraries because it was free for nonprofits for a maximum of four hours. Unfortunately, as the years went by, space became limited and our meeting dates had to shift, creating inconsistency. Our membership started to decline, so we started getting worried because we could not serve our members without a location to meet and with so many inconsistent dates and times. Of course, it gets worse, we faced the worst situation that I had always feared. The original co-founder decided that it was too much for her to handle as she was also in the process of selling her house and moving away. I never imagined that she would walk away; nor had I planned for how to support the organization alone. Remember she approached me to start this nonprofit.

Just like that, I found myself running the organization alone. I told the co-founder that she needed to show up at a meeting to share the news with the girls because she owed them that much and it was not my responsibility to make the announcement. I was so disappointed, hurt, frustrated, and scared; but mostly I feared disappointing the girls with possibly having to dismantle the organization. Remember my story, I lost and missed out on so much in my childhood; that was a major trigger for me. This situation took me back to my own childhood, as I was trying to figure things out. I spent time praying on it and I thought about one of the parents that was so helpful and committed to the organization. She was very hands-on and had some great ideas, so I decided to approach her to see if she would be interested in becoming a part of the leadership team with me. I had heard it said that those who may be best suited for a position are those you least expect. That is when God answered my prayer, she said yes! She is now the Chief Operating Officer and financially vested as well! Praise God, I am no longer alone; however, there was so much that she did not know about nonprofits and I was still learning myself.

I am still fearful of us not being able to stay afloat and create a structure to support the success of the organization. Oh, I did not tell you that I am a big dreamer as well, so that was my fear, that my big dreams and plans, I had for the organization would not come to pass. The new COO and I were meeting one day, trying to understand what needed to be done for the organization from an administrative, financial, and legal standpoint. To our distress, we discovered that there were no documents or records kept; just a binder with papers and voided checks! Thankfully, we went through a training a year or so prior and I was able to reach out to that nonprofit consultant to get some advice, as well as worked with our local nonprofit institute to get us on track with all the proper paperwork and filings. We also learned about more nonprofit resources that were available to us. I was determined to not let the devil win this fight; especially at the expense of the young women in the organization. I had been in this for two years now and the girls had been sharing and opening up so much about their pains, challenges, and goals that they wanted to accomplish. I had never experienced this, remember I did not have what I was offering them. Hearing and knowing what their hearts were going through and yearning to do, I could not destroy the "safe space" that I promised and created for them. I had to push through all my fears, anger of being left behind, and disappointment by others. I did not know what was next, but I realized that I had to move from leading with my heart and really tap into using my head. I had to save this safe space that I had created for these young women.

I continued the journey of tapping into my resources. I realized that because I had walked most of my life's journey alone, I must now find the courage and strength to trust and be open to the reality that God has people for me. I must continue to ask and pray that He brings the right people that are willing to support me in bringing my mission and vision to life. I was in the midst of running for public office and I was invited to speak at a PTO meeting where they asked me to speak about my nonprofit and so I did. After the meeting, a parent approached me and inquired about how she can get involved in the organization. We scheduled an interview and things went amazingly well. In 2018 that parent joined and has been a blessing to the organization, serving as our Director of Program Management. We now are moving on up like the Jeffersons!

I started feeling like God is truly listening and answering my prayers, so I took another leap of faith. As you will remember, one of my organizational obstacles was securing a location to keep our membership stable and growing. I decided to post a call-to-action on Facebook to see if there was anyone that would be willing to donate meeting space to a local nonprofit. Mind you, I do not like asking, nor like people in my business. I reminded myself that this nonprofit mission is not about me, it was solely about continuing to provide a safe space for these girls. Oh, by the way, one of those girls is my one and only daughter!

Phenomenal Young Women Inc. is creating a sisterhood and a family for my daughter, just in case God decides to call me home. I wanted her to have everything that I did not have, even a homemade family that will love her unconditionally just like me. My call-to-action Facebook post got a hit! A local business owner was interested in possibly offering us space. She wanted to schedule some time to discuss the details and our needs. Can I tell you all that God is so good! She offered us a beautiful space that felt like home and we got to be there for eight months straight. This place was such a blessing. Our membership grew so much we were packing in the space like a can of sardines! My heart was full. We had amazing guest speakers that the girls were really connecting with and asking, "Can we bring them back?" I could not have asked for anything more!

You know with every high moment comes a low moment, right? After such an amazing time in our location, we had a bomb dropped on us. It was good news and bad news! The donor of the location was moving her business outside of the county, so the location was shutting down. What a bummer. However, we were so grateful to her pouring into our organization and we were happy and supportive of her new business venture. Oh, and by the way, her daughter is a member of our organization now! We had to go back to using the local libraries and risk losing members due to the library's unstable booking dates. And we did! We dealt with that for quite some time in 2019 until one of our amazing parents offered us the opportunity to utilize a local Charming Charlie's location that had recently closed. We took a break in January every year to plan our new year, especially due to weather being an issue during that time.

In September, I did another big thing! I took another leap of faith and started interviewing for my first set of Board of Directors for the organization. After a series of interviews, we finalized the final five board members in December of 2019. We hosted our annual new year open house and announce our amazing new location and introduced, and installed our new Board of Directors. We had a great turnout at our open house and quite a few new member registrations. We had a few meetings in our new space and of course, COVID-19 happened here in 2020. As we all know now, COVID required lots of pivoting for business owners, nonprofits, and families. We decided to convert our programming to virtual in order to maintain a sense of normalcy and connection for the girls. We hosted a parent meeting to get everyone's feedback and to ensure that the parents were a part of the decision-making since it is their precious jewels that we serve.

Now that we are in a pandemic state, it continues to create new challenges. Parents are overwhelmed with work, homeschooling, and trying to find balance. Unfortunately, many are not communicating in a way that will allow us to serve them effectively, in the virtual capacity. Nonetheless, we continue to move forward with the ones that show up and serve them at the same level of excellence each time. The nonprofit journey of community service has been a heavy load to bear, however, when you continue to focus on your *why*, your mission, your vision, and the people you serve, it gives you what you need to keep pushing.

I realized that God covered me through it all. When I was going through the journey in fear, frustration, and hurt, God sent angels my way in 2019 and 2020 to support me. Through this process, God allowed me to become a four-time award-winning Nonprofit Executive of the Year. It is amazing to know that even in the valley you can be seen and appreciated for the work that you do. I am so grateful for regaining my power and strength to continue to serve and pour into young women. I know that there will be more obstacles ahead, but I will always remember to embrace my resilience to empower excellence as I continue to serve! I want you to do the same *Legacy Leader!*

Personal Reflections/Notes
Nonprofit Wisdom & Insights

A COMPILATION OF NONPROFIT EXPERTS

THANK YOU

THANK YOU TO EACH NONPROFIT LEGACY CO-AUTHOR FOR YOUR DEDICATION AND CONTRIBUTION TO THIS PROJECT!

TAJALA BATTLE-LOCKHART

FEATURED NONPROFIT ORGANIZATIONS:

Featured Nonprofit Organizations

Phenomenal Young Women, Inc
Category: Young Women Development
Name: Tajala Battle-Lockhart
Phone Number: 240-903-0103
Email: pywmaryland@gmail.com
Website: www.phenomenalyoungwomen.org
Facebook: www.facebook.com/phenomenalyoungwomen
Twitter: @pywmd
Instagram: @pywmd

Tilted Crowns Inc
Category: Young Women Development
Name: Allison Bryant
Phone Number: 727-743-4520
Email: abryant@tiltedcrowns.net
Website: www.tiltedcrowns.org
Facebook: www.facebook.com/tiltedcrownsinc
Instagram: tilted_crowns_inc

PEARLS OF PURPOSE INC
Category: Women & Girls at Risk
Name: Chemeka Turner Williams
Phone Number: 919-943-8086
Email: chemekaturnerwilliams@gmail.com
Website: www.chemekaturnerwilliams.com
Facebook: @pearlsofpurposeinc
Instagram: @Chemeka Turner-Williams

Accessibility Bridge
Category: Disability, Inclusion
Name: Dee Sapp
Phone: 202.871.5522
Email: dsapp@accessibilitybridge.com
Website: www.accessibilitybridge.com
Facebook: www.facebook.com/accessbridge
Twitter: @accessbridgesco
Mailing Address: 4660 Crain Hwy, #1622, White Plains, MD 20695

SISTERS LIFTING SISTERS INC
Category: Women & Youth at Risk
Name: Erica Perry Green
Phone Number: 919-522-8195
Email: slsempowerment@gmail.com
Website: www.sistersliftingsisters.org
Facebook: www.facebook.com/SistersLiftingSistersSLS
Instagram: @sistersliftingsisters

IT TAKES TWO, INC
Category: Youth Development
Name: Jaemellah Kemp
Phone: 443.302.9799
Email: jkemp@ittakestwoinc.org
Website: www.ittakestwoinc.org
Facebook: www.facebook.com/ittakestwoinc
Instagram: @ittakestwoinc
LinkedIn: https://www.linkedin.com/company/it-takes-two
Mailing Address: PO Box 787 Gambrills, MD 21236

STELLA'S GIRL INC
Category: International Women Development and International Youth Development
Name: Kaprece James
Phone Number: 912-596-7937
Email: programs@stellasgirls.org
Website: www.stellasgirls.org
Facebook: www.facebook.com/stellasgirlsinc
Twitter: @stellasgirlsinc
Instagram: @stellasgirlsinc
Mailing Address: 7455 Sandy Bottom Ct Hughesville MD 20637

Beautiful Butterflies, Inc.
Category: Invisible Illness/Health and Wellness
Name: Keva Brooks Napper
Phone Number: 336-528-4224
Email: beautifulbutterfliesinc11@gmail.com
Website: www.mybeautifulbutterflies.com
Facebook: www.facebook.com/mybeautifulbutterflies
Twitter: @my_bbi
Instagram: @my_bbi
Mailing Address: P.O. Box 164, Sedalia, NC 27432

Gurls EmPOWERment Network
Category: Young & Women Development
Name: Kiwan N. Fitch-Webster
Phone: 803-609-3408
Email: gurlsempowermentsc@gmail.com
CoachK@J2Pglobalinstitute.com
Facebook: www.facebook.com/gurlsempowermentnetwork
Twitter: @gurlsnetwork
Instagram: @gurlsempowermentnetwork
Mailing Address: 1726 Sumter St. Columbia SC 29201

Beyond the Classroom, Inc.
Category: Youth Development
Name: Lisa Ambers
Phone Number: 703-999-4416
Email: info@beyondtheclassroominc.org
Website: www.beyondtheclassroominc.org
Facebook: www.facebook.com/beyondtheclassroominc
Twitter: @ClassroomInc
Instagram: @btc_nonprofit
Mailing Address: 9464 Biltmore Street, Waldorf, MD 20603

Girl Noticed, Inc.
Category: Art and Activism
Name: Lori Pratico
Phone Number: 954-605-5208
Email: info@girlnoticed.org
Website: www.girlnoticed.org
Facebook: www.facebook.com/girlnoticed
Twitter: @girlnoticed
Instagram: @girlnoticed
Mailing Address: 1350 East Sunrise Blvd. Ste 110, Fort Lauderdale, FL 33304

National Nonprofit Minority Association
Category: Nonprofit Associations
Name: Dr Rhonika Thomas
Phone: 314-677-1006
Website: President@nationalnonprofitminorityassociation.com
www.nationalnonprofitminorityassociation.org
Facebook: www.facebook.com/NationalNonprofitMinorityAssociation/
Instagram: www.instagram.com/nonproftminorityassociation

LifeStyles of Maryland Foundation, Inc
Category: People in Crisis
Name: Sandy Washington
Phone: 301-645-2933
Website: www.lifestylesofmd.org/
Facebook: www.facebook.com/lifestylesofmaryland
Mailing Address: 101 Catalpa Drive, Suite 103, La Plata, MD 20646

Girl Speak Inc.
Category: Youth Female Empowerment & Enrichment
Name: Sharon Y. Anderson
Phone Number: 301.717.3410
Email: girlspeaklife@gmailcom
Website: girlspeakinc.org
Facebook: www.facebook.com/girlspeaklife
Twitter: @girlspeakinc
Instagram: @girl_speak_inc
Mailing Address: P.O. Box 196 Suitland, MD 20752-0196
Office: Creative Suitland Art Center 4719 Silver Hill Road, Suitland, Maryland, 20746

THE NONPROFIT LEGACY BUSINESS DIRECTORY:

The Nonprofit Legacy Business Directory

Jaemellah Kemp Consulting, LLC
Category: Nonprofit Start Up, Board Development
Name: Jaemellah Kemp
Phone: 410.831.0829
Website: www.jaemellahkempconsulting.com
Facebook: www.facebook.com/jaemellahkempconsulting
Instagram: @jaemellahkempconsulting

Journey Towards Purpose Global Institute
Category: Coaching and Consulting
Name: Kiwan N. Fitch-Webster (Please update if not correct)
Phone: 803-609-3408
Email: CoachK@J2Pglobalinstitute.com
Facebook: www.facebook.com/J2PGlobalinstitute
Twitter: @KiwanFitch
Instagram: @Kiwanfitch
Mailing Address: 1726 Sumter St. Columbia, SC 29201

Ty Boone Enterprises
Category: Nonprofit /Grants Management Consulting
Name: Tykeysha Boone
Phone Number: 800-647-4877
Email: tykeysha@tybooneenterprises.com
Website: www.tybooneconsulting.com
Facebook: www.facebook.com/tybooneconsulting
Twitter: @tybooneconsulting
Instagram: @tybooneconsulting
Mailing Address: 459 Main Street, 101-273 Trussville, AL 35173

TAJ Consulting & Events
Category: Consulting/Coaching
Name: Tajala Lockhart
Phone: 240-903-0103
Website: www.tajconsultingevents.com
Facebook: www.facebook.com/tajconsultingevents
Instagram: @tajconsultingevents

Divine Nonprofit Solutions LLC
Category: QuickBooks/Bookkeeping
Name: Vina McRay
Phone: (833) 600-0569
Email: info@divinenonprofits.com
Website: https://divinenonprofits.com/

ACHI Magazine
Category: Biannual Digital and Print Magazine and Awards Show
Name: Dr Juanita Fletcher, Editor-N-Chief, Taneisha Fletcher, Creative Editor
Phone Number: 1-844-588-ACHI
Email: achimagazine@wswassociation.com
Website: www.achimagazine.com
Facebook: www.facebook.com/ACHIMagazine
Instagram: @achimagazine
Mailing Address: 400 Pryor St., SW, #4652 Atlanta, GA 30302

ACHI Women Supporting Women Inc
Category: Faith Based & Women owned / Supporting Women & Girls
Name: Kimberly Tetterton, National Director
Phone Number: 1-844-588-ACHI
Email: members@wswassociation.com
Website: www.wswassociation.com
Facebook: www.facebook.com/ACHIWSWANational
Instagram: @achiwswa
Mailing Address: 400 Pryor St., SW, #4652 Atlanta, GA 30302

Stay in Compliance, Accounting and Bookkeeping Services
Category: Compliance/Accounting/Finance
Name: Kenya R. Thomas, M. Ed
Phone Number: 314-584-9140
Email: Stayincomply@gmail.com
Facebook: www.facebook.com/stayincompliance
Mailing Address: 3725 Estates Drive, Florissant, MO. 63033

We are not guaranteeing services however providing quality resources that can support you on your journey.

Please share with these business owner's that The Nonprofit Legacy sent you their way. Wishing you much success on your journey!

A COMPILATION OF NONPROFIT EXPERTS

THE NONPROFIT LEGACY

TAJALA BATTLE-LOCKHART

TAJ CONSULTING & EVENTS SPONSORED
AND HOSTED THIS COMPILATION TO SHOW
NONPROFIT LEADERS ADDITIONAL WAYS TO
CREATE EARNED INCOME OPPORTUNITIES
FOR THIER ORGANIZATIONS.

"CREATING SOLUTIONS
THAT CREATE PROFITS."

EXPOSURE, VALUE, ACCOUNTABILITY = RESULTS

T A J C O N S U L T I N G E V E N T S . C O M

shero *publishing*

Made in the USA
Columbia, SC
16 October 2020

22956651R00089